The Art of Strategic Leadership

The Art of Strategic Leadership

Lynn L. Adams, David A. Jochim and Thomas R. Cutting

R.W. Beck, Inc.

The Art of Strategic Leadership
Copyright © 2008 Lynn L. Adams, David A. Jochim and Thomas R. Cutting
Published by R.W. Beck, Inc.

This publication is designed to provide accurate and authoritative information in regard to the subject matter covered. It is sold with the understanding that neither the author nor the publisher is engaged in rendering financial, accounting, legal, or other professional services by publishing this book. If financial advice or other expert assistance is needed, the service of a competent professional should be sought. The author and publisher specifically disclaim any liability, loss or risk resulting from the use or application of the information contained in this book.

For more information, please contact:
ladams@rwbeck.com

Book design by:
Arbor Books, Inc.
www.arborbooks.com

Printed in Canada

The Art of Strategic Leadership
Lynn L. Adams, David A. Jochim and Thomas R. Cutting

1. Title 2. Author 3. Management and Leadership

Library of Congress Control Number: 2008924253

ISBN 10: 0-9816327-0-X
ISBN 13: 978-0-9816327-0-4

Table of Contents

Preface

Over the years we have completed numerous engagements where we helped clients work through difficult organizational and/or leadership issues. Often, after a particularly long day, we would find ourselves in a spirited dinner discussion about writing a book on strategic leadership. Because we work primarily for public and private infrastructure organizations responsible for delivering energy and water services, we were especially intrigued with the concept of writing a book that would help them think and act more strategically.

It is no secret that infrastructure organizations across the country are faced with huge problems. Baby boomers are retiring and there is a much smaller supply of talent to replace them; organizations are faced with looming capital needs but lack resources to manage and implement projects; and boards across the country are demanding greater efficiency from the organizations they oversee. It's not that infrastructure organizations haven't thought about these problems—they have. Many even have some sort of strategic plan on file somewhere. Typically, we find these plans are referenced infrequently if at all, few people within the organizations know they exist, and they are often viewed as "management's plan."

Strategic leadership gets talked about, written about and worried about, but ultimately it is rather elusive. The old adage *simple but not easy* applies well. We know when we see strong leadership, but we don't necessarily know how to achieve it. We grant that there are certain innate characteristics that good leaders share; however, there are also tools and techniques to be studied and applied that contribute to the mix. We are focused on those leaders who rise up through our working organizations and are charged with leading, often in roles they never consciously sought but instead grew into, often from a technical background.

This book then has been written for those of us who are responsible for day-to-day leadership of organizations. Our challenge is not typically the technical content of our organization's work; our challenge is strategically leading the organization through the ever-constant challenges and opportunities that it faces. In short, the soft stuff is really the hard stuff.

When someone is not sure whether their organization would benefit from an organized approach to strategic leadership, we like to ask: What are your organization's top three strategic initiatives for this year? How were those identified? Does everyone in your organization know what they are? If answering these questions makes you uneasy, we think the ideas and processes contained in this book can benefit your organization. Change will happen. It's a fact. There are only two choices: Either lead change or change will control your organization.

—Lynn Adams, David Jochim and Tom Cutting
January 2008

1

Introduction
A Need for Change

History is full of examples of outstanding leadership. We all know them and have studied many, from great political and wartime leaders to outstanding heads of multinational corporations. Books abound documenting the lives and successful traits of people who have led great armies during times of crisis, spearheaded great industrial or technological advances, inspired fundamental cultural change, or provided leadership on the sports field.

This book has been written for the vast majority of us who will never be sports icons or lead great armies, but who are responsible for day-to-day leadership of public and private infrastructure organizations that deliver water, energy and transportation services. We, too, are responsible for driving organizational improvement and change. The most challenging aspect of our jobs as we become leaders is typically not the technical content of what our organization does or produces. It is strategically leading the organization through the ever-constant challenges and opportunities that seem to crop up at an astonishing pace. In short, the soft stuff is really the hard stuff.

The focus of this book is how to recognize, adapt, plan and act as an integrated organization to address these changes. One key job of true leadership is to move from fragmentation to integration, providing coherence and context for the daily swirl of activities. The ability to integrate and adapt to change on a consistent basis is what separates true organizational leaders from technical managers.

Academic institutions and business schools teem with theories on how to address such issues and develop the kind of organization that is able to thrive in the midst of changing demands. Although a more academic context can be useful, the approach outlined here is different in some very key ways. *The Art of Strategic Leadership* focuses on the practical and pragmatic by minding some basic organizational truths and outlining a process that enables leaders to function effectively—despite obstacles—and organizations to have the clarity of direction and accountability necessary to make change.

From the boardroom to the field, the vast majority of organizations operating in infrastructure markets historically have had a low tolerance for change and an even lower appreciation for anything that includes the word "strategic." It is no wonder. Many of these organizations have experienced "strategic planning," typically when a near meltdown occurred or on a routine annual basis like clockwork, efforts that resulted in little or no substantive long-term change. Add to this the disillusioning fact that the planning was often done by a limited group of people disconnected from the staff, management and governing body. The resulting negative connotation attached to the word "strategic" in many organizations raises the question of why we would choose to include it in our title. That is a fair question.

Webster's Dictionary defines strategic as *"of great importance within an integrated whole or to a planned effort."* Strategic leadership done properly implies an ability to proactively lead with an eye to the future and to do so with a clear awareness of the integrated whole. Webster's further defines art as *"the conscious use of skill and creative imagination."* This book, then, is about strategic leadership: how to work with—even inspire—other human beings internal and external to an organization to help them think strategically and work together in teams to achieve an often challenging common direction.

Achieving success within an organization typically requires working with others to identify and achieve common direction and goals. Experience has shown that this often entails *"the conscious use of skill and creative imagination"*—hence more of an art form than the application of a structured process or a science.

The Art of Strategic Leadership is about how to use skill and creative imagination to apply a toolkit of processes and techniques to lead an organization—including board, management and staff—through a process that results in defining and achieving a common strategic direction. Emphasis on achieving the desired direction is key. Some of the changes will happen during the process itself, but there are specific and intentional approaches that make this more effective and increase the likelihood that actual implementation will occur. In short, *The Art of Strategic Leadership* describes a process that creates a sustainable, programmatic approach to strategy and leadership.

Strategic leadership entails more than only the board, senior management and key staff members—it must occur at all levels of the organization. Making this happen requires harnessing three critical elements:

- **Future Focus** requires looking well beyond day-to-day operational issues. The governing body and senior management must provide this critical input.

- **Operational Imperatives** that impact the organization must be identified and channeled to drive the process of change forward.
- **Organizational Alignment** focuses on creating an organization that is well adapted to its purposes and strategic direction with all components in place and functioning effectively.

Elements of Strategic Leadership

Defining Your Direction

For every organization embarking on a path of change, the General Manager (GM) or Chief Executive Officer (CEO), along with the board, must think strategically with a focus on the long-term future and create a sense of urgency early in the change process. Thinking strategically does not occur naturally in many organizations, especially those that are dealing with day-to-day operational issues and "putting out fires." These hardworking individuals often have little time to devote to identifying and solving the organization's strategic issues. Without such a longer term focus, an organization is destined to perpetuate the same missteps that inhibit progress, create organizational frustration and result in less than optimal effectiveness.

The Art of Strategic Leadership introduces proven processes and techniques to help boards and senior management think strategically. This is especially true in the public sector and, depending on circumstances, to a great extent in the private sector. The board, because it is ultimately responsible for the performance and activities of the organization, plays a critical role in providing the big picture strategic direction for the organization. The role of the board is so important—and usually misunderstood—that we have devoted the last chapter of this book to it.

The responsibility for thinking strategically does not rest solely on the board's shoulders, but is in fact a shared responsibility among the board, executive leadership, senior management and staff. How to get the entire organization to think and act strategically is one hallmark of *The Art of Strategic Leadership*. Of equal value, this book also shows how to develop strategic leadership throughout the organization and demonstrates how participation in the change process provides for the nurturing and cultivation of future leaders. This last element—cultivating future leaders—has become increasingly important with shifting workplace demographics.

Energizing the Organization

Most organizations have a continual need to deal with new and sometimes complex issues that may originate from internal or external sources. A wide array of models and techniques is available to help organizations discover and implement solutions. Over the last decade, bookshelves have filled with a variety of business management books and publications. Many are published by those in academia, others by active or retired executives and managers. Most of these books contain pearls of wisdom and theories that may apply in specific situations.

As we spend time with organizations across the country and elsewhere around the world we continually hear several common themes: "Nothing ever changes," "We've done this before," and "What is going to be different *this* time?"

The Art of Strategic Leadership offers a practical solution to dealing with organizational issues that arise from the business challenges constantly facing an organization. Rather than offering a snapshot solution for organizations facing particular issues and challenges at a particular point in time, it offers a process for organizational improvement that is dynamic yet straightforward. Most important, it aligns the full organization so that the desired and agreed upon direction can be implemented. Once learned and applied in an organizational setting, it will equip leaders with an effective tool for creating a flexible, fluid organization that is aligned with its purpose.

Focusing on Change

Organizations operate in a sea of change: Markets shift. Staff composition changes. Technology accelerates. Costs increase. Budgets are stressed. People are retiring. Recruiting needs are increasing. Training is vital. Regulations are in flux. All of this creates the constant challenge of change for an organization. Nothing about the changes in the environment organizations exist in is unusual, except that maybe the pace of change has quickened as technology and society move more and more into real-time issues and response.

Addressing change is much like navigating a ship through storms, crosswinds, and calm seas, or flying a plane through changing weather. The imperative in these cases is that navigation must dynamically respond to the changes in the environment.

Add to this business reality the fact that many people—particularly those who are attracted to engineering and scientific disciplines—suffer from some degree of *novophobia*. That is, there is an innate resistance to change—and in some people an outright fear of change—that runs counter to the demands of today's business environment. This novophobia contributes to the difficulty leaders have in aligning their organization with the demanding tasks at hand.

In fact, some resistance to change can be an asset and contribute to creating a healthy organizational tension; this is true only if enough of a counterbalancing, risk-friendly orientation is in place. However, most infrastructure organizations tend to be more risk averse, creating a need for specific attention in this area. In response to this dominant organizational profile, *The Art of Strategic Leadership* builds acceptance for change through a cross-organizational process that features specific techniques to deal with novophobia.

Navigating through Change

Strategic leadership is about recognition that the organization operates in an environment of change. It is about equipping leadership with the tools to efficiently navigate the organization in response to change. It is about developing the organizational culture that expects change, responds to change, and even proactively changes in anticipation of future trends affecting the organization's business.

Consider the earlier example of an airplane pilot in changing weather conditions. On a cross-country flight the pilot might encounter strong headwinds, requiring an adjustment to fuel needs, arrival times, or a host of other items. Upon encountering strong crosswinds, a heading adjustment might be warranted. A major thunderstorm might require plotting a detour, or a change in waypoint or arrival destination. Should these things materialize, does the pilot reverse course and go back to his starting place and give up? No, his expectation from the outset was that these kinds of changes are just part of flying. He is trained to respond to these changes in the environment. He very likely has tools and technology, such as autopilot or weather radar, to help respond to the variable conditions.

What if your organization was built on a culture that expected and adapted to change quickly and efficiently? Further, what if your organization had tools and processes that were embedded into management, staff and decision makers that enabled efficient adaptation to change? This book provides those tools and processes, and while it is far from an autopilot, it does give executives, managers, staff and governing bodies comfort in the organization's ability to adapt and flourish in a changing environment. Strategic leaders will instill such tools and process into the organization. They will understand that an organization must constantly adapt and develop the capability to lead itself to a culture that expects change, not just responds to it. *The Art of Strategic Leadership* produces real change because it equips organizations with this understanding and will create the organizational change necessary to adapt to the demands of today's business environment.

Organizational Need

As management consultants, for many years we have worked with a variety of organizations in various locations around the world. We have found no single common denominator that characterizes the challenges facing the average organization; organizational need varies considerably across the range of possibilities. Some organizations operate in near paralysis because of labor-related issues or major disconnects between their board, management and staff. Others lack a sense of direction and purpose. Still others are experiencing a drain of institutional knowledge with no clear solution. Many have communications issues that hamper both effective leadership and the ability of staff to follow. These are just a few examples of the challenges uncovered.

The problem that remains for most public and private organizations operating in infrastructure businesses, including water, transportation, and energy, is that no comprehensive, flexible approach for building strategic leadership has existed within the organization. In today's business environment, every organization must be competitive, either on a regional or global basis. This book provides that approach. It describes proven processes that can meet the needs of any organization, public or private, large or small, regardless of the organization's current level of fitness. The principles contained in this book apply to organizations located in industrialized nations. They also apply to organizations that are based in developing countries, especially emerging economies. Often, these organizations are struggling to overcome the effects of social, economic and religious traditions in order to become players in world markets, improve environmental conditions, utilize new technologies or become compliant with international standards. Rather than becoming another flavor of the month, the principles and activities contained in this book will influence for good the culture of the organization that will have a lasting impact.

"The department was in jeopardy of being dismantled by the county. It was our ability to explain the strategic leadership process we were engaged in that gave us the time we needed to make real change."
—Board Chair of a County Water Department

Grounding Change in Reality

The approaches and techniques presented here are based on real experiences with real organizations struggling with real challenges in their daily business. All individuals and the organizations they work for must deal with change. As Spencer Johnson suggests in his book *Who Moved My Cheese?*, change happens, regardless of how hard we try to prevent it. Keeping the process for change grounded in reality is important. The organization must continue to reliably fulfill its core business responsibilities of delivering power, water and the like at the same time staff members are engaged in implementing strategic initiatives.

As noted earlier, numerous books and other publications have been written that offer valuable theories, techniques, tools and processes to address strategy and leadership issues in the workplace. Among them are three books that have stood the test of time: *Good To Great*, by Jim Collins; *Reinventing Your Board*, by John Carver; and *Leading Change*, by John P. Kotter. *The Art of Strategic Leadership* incorporates ideas contained in these books and highly recommends those as required reading from the long list of available business texts.

Anticipation of Change

Strategic leaders do more than *respond to change* and reactively—even reluctantly—move their organizations to address these changes. Strategic leaders have become comfortable with change; they have become comfortable with the tools to help their organizations change. Indeed, such leaders *expect change*, just as the pilot in the earlier example expects to deal with changing weather conditions.

True strategic leaders do still more. As they become more and more comfortable with the constantly changing business environment and are armed with a process to flexibly adapt their organizations to these changes, the expectation of change begins to evolve into an *anticipation of change*. Achieving this level of comfort with change, both environmental and organizational, is the hallmark of a strategic leader.

Anticipation of change is not meant to indicate an excitement surrounding simply the process of dealing with organizational change for its own sake. It is more; it is about building the essential skills and positioning of the organization for this change ahead of its occurrence—that is, involving the organization proactively rather than simply reactively. Leadership within an organization that has reached this level of familiarity and understanding has clearly become strategic.

In addition to planning, these principles apply broadly to a variety of situations. *The Art of Strategic Leadership* techniques have been used to:

- Integrate corporate sustainability efforts
- Facilitate conflict resolution
- Increase effectiveness of functional units or work teams
- Assemble and consolidate project teams
- Direct specific task assignments
- Develop risk management strategies
- Launch public relations or sales campaigns
- Communicate effectively with boards and senior management

- Design and implement public involvement campaigns
- Work with external stakeholder groups

Application of the logical and straightforward techniques contained in this book will develop skills needed to understand and prioritize issues, effectively lead the organization, and, most importantly, gain full endorsement from senior management, staff and board members.

Assessing Organizational Need

There are several simple prompts that can identify whether the organization is in need of improved strategic leadership and is a good candidate for change. For example:

- Are you having trouble delivering basic services while building for the future?
- Is your organization mired in internal battles?
- Do you wonder how to achieve an enhanced external/customer focus?
- Is there a sense of a leadership void, often associated with low morale?
- Are you responding to the following:
    - Staff is not clear on where the organization is heading
    - Board, management and staff do not have a clear and productive working relationship
    - We operate in silos with lots of attention to divisions
    - We lack a common unifying goal
    - Accountability is lacking
    - We cannot implement our capital improvement plan
    - Many key employees are retiring
    - We have not captured institutional knowledge
    - The organization is ineffective
    - We don't know how to make decisions
    - My board is micromanaging
    - We don't communicate well within the organization

- Operations and engineering don't communicate effectively
- We do not have strong customer relations
- We are not getting our work done

All of these items are symptoms of an organization that is being challenged. Rather than deal with these items randomly and in a disconnected manner, *The Art of Strategic Leadership* describes processes that will help the entire organization understand and address them in an integrated fashion with a prioritized and specific implementation approach.

One Simple Test

If it is unclear whether or not an organization could benefit from an integrated approach to strategic leadership, just ask: *What are the organization's top three strategic initiatives for this year and why? Does the entire organization know what they are?* If you or the members of your organization cannot clearly answer these questions, you will benefit from a number of the ideas and processes contained in this book. The fact is that change will happen. There are only two choices: Either lead it or it will control your organization.

THE THREE MOST IMPORTANT ISSUES

As at many business retreats, the chief operating officer of a large water agency invited a guest speaker from a large water agency across the state to spend a few hours talking about a topic of interest. At the conclusion of the speaker's remarks, questions were invited from the assembled group. Most were somewhat generic in nature, in other words real yawners. The last question came from the facilitator: "What are your three most important issues?" Within a few nanoseconds and to the complete amazement of his audience, the guest speaker passionately hammered home his three issues, which included institutional knowledge concerns and future water supply shortages. Once he departed the meeting, the facilitator turned to the remaining chief operating officer and asked, "What are YOUR three most important issues?" Although he was unable to articulate an answer until weeks later, the lesson learned is that every manager AND his or her staff should know the three top issues facing the organization, and that the issues should be identical! Change is more likely to occur if everyone is on the same page.

2

Framework
Setting the Stage
for Change

In order to effectively use the process and approach described in *The Art of Strategic Leadership*, a solid framework must first be established. Attitudes, behaviors, leadership skills, common understanding and business acumen are a few of the important framework components that must be in place in order to build your strategic leadership and to set the stage for change in the organization.

Setting the stage for change entails a number of initial steps. This section describes how to accomplish the following items at the beginning of the process:

- Identify a Change Agent
- Announce a call to action
- Study the process and terminology
- Appoint a Core Planning Team
- Produce a planning schedule
- Read reference books
- Appoint a facilitator

Strategic Leaders as Change Agents

Although obvious when stated, but often overlooked or minimized, the first step to creating change in any organization is for someone to acknowledge the need for change—that the status quo is not acceptable. The ideal situation is for the key strategic leader in the organization to function as the Change Agent. Optimally, the chief executive (General Manager or Chief Executive Officer) fulfills this role and, after consulting with others, clearly announces the need for change. This announcement, in essence a call to action, must be presented with conviction and accompanied by a clear and demonstrable sense of urgency. If the urgency aspect of the message is missing, staff will have little motivation to get on board. If the organization is large, the Change Agent may be a division manager or equivalent, ideally with support and backing from his or her superior, although in reality this is not always the case.

Across organizations, Change Agents have certain attributes in common. They are likely to exhibit the following attributes and traits:

- Skilled communicators, both written and verbal
- Lead by example
- Generate interest and enthusiasm
- Impatient with status quo

- Able to see the big picture
- Attuned to interpersonal dynamics
- Risk takers
- Forthright but diplomatic

Other Leaders as Change Agents

The very nature of understanding the need for and being willing to champion organizational change designates an individual as a Change Agent. Although often these people are at the top of an organization, sometimes they are found elsewhere.

There are many situations when the GM/CEO does not see, acknowledge or agree with the need for change. Although the ideal situation involves alignment for change at the executive ranks, sometimes organizational change needs to begin at a more grassroots level. In this approach, a department or division can initiate change, keep superiors informed and remain open to their more active participation down the road. This allows energy to build that the rest of the organization cannot deny and that may ultimately result in organization-wide buy-in. This approach by definition identifies emerging leaders who may be less senior in the organization and can be thought of as "leading by example."

In this situation—you see the need for change but are not part of the top executive staff—how do you convince the organizational leadership that change is necessary? One approach builds on the organizational change prompts listed at the end of Chapter 1. Opening a dialog with these questions will build understanding—or at least plant seeds for later development—with key stakeholders and leaders within the organization.

GETTING THE GM/CEO ON BOARD

A dialog between the Change Agent and the GM/CEO may go something like this:

Change Agent: I noted at your last all-hands briefing that you used the word "change" several times and I wanted to ask you more about that. I have also been thinking about this recently. Could you tell me more about what is on your mind in that regard?

GM/CEO: It's fairly clear that staff is overwhelmed and we are not on track to implement our capital improvement plan. Plus, it's clear that many of our managers are reluctant to make decisions and the board is micromanaging. I'd like to build an organization that could be effective over the long term and I think that's going to require change.

Change Agent: So, not implementing the capital improvement plan, managers who are not as effective as they could be and a micromanaging board are the top three concerns on your mind?

GM/CEO: Those three plus a few others, like the brain drain that is happening as baby boomers retire.

Change Agent: I have been having similar thoughts and was reviewing some parts of *Leading Change* by John Kotter where he talks about the job of leadership being to create a vision and move toward it despite the obstacles. Would you be interested in some ideas on how we might make the organizational changes necessary to be more effective?

GM/CEO: Well, yes, but I don't want to waste time and money on a process that goes nowhere.

Change Agent: I understand and fully agree. How urgent do you think this is?

GM/CEO: It's keeping me awake at night, so it would be good to start making some changes sooner rather than later.

Change Agent: Let me do some research to gather up some ideas and we can talk later this week.

The bottom line is that if you are not one of the senior executives of an organization, your role as citing the need and urgency for organizational change will of necessity become somewhat of a sales job. This means the obligation falls on you to understand key organizational issues and build an effective message that builds buy-in *up* the organizational hierarchy. The aspiring Change Agent could develop an entire presentation focused on the need for organizational change using this methodology.

Why Become a Change Agent?

Sometimes, you simply cannot help yourself. If you are reading this book, it is very likely that you are now or aspire to become a true strategic leader and Change Agent—it is how your brain is wired. Change Agents exhibit those common traits outlined previously that predispose them to observe the need for organizational change and feel inspired to act. In addition, Change Agents are high-impact players in their organizations. By the nature of what they do, they are key to organizational movement and success; this often leads to career opportunities and advancement. In fact, we know of several ex-employees who have been specifically sought out by organizations to return with an acknowledged role of creating change. And we have observed senior recruitments where the final decision rested on which candidate would be the most effective Change Agent. This represents growing recognition and high praise indeed for the impact of such a role within an organization.

Getting Staff on Board

Once the Change Agent has self-identified—either at the executive level or somewhere else in the organization—and built the leadership buy-in necessary, the next step is to announce the intended change to the broader organization. This is an important step and must revolve around a message that is clear, universally understood and compelling. The point of this step is to alert staff that change is coming and to start the process of building broad endorsement of the need for and the specific plan for change. This falls into the "no surprises" model of leadership and creates transparency. Such a transparent leadership approach accomplishes several key missions:

- Shows respect for your staff
- Incorporates staff ideas from the start
- Starts to build broad organizational buy-in
- Frames involvement in implementation efforts
- Foreshadows that change is coming, allowing time to accept the idea
- Limits water cooler gossip by taking control of the message
- Builds morale

The initial statement is important as it sets the tone of urgency. For example, a typical announcement for a utility might be, "Operating costs are too high. Within the next year, we must identify the means necessary to work smarter without requiring approval of higher utility rates." Another example: "Our customers demand a higher degree of sustainability. We must embark on an approach to integrate and expand such efforts."

Often the essence of the message of urgency can be found in the vision, mission or strategic direction statement as already framed by the organization. Although further validation of such statements is an essential step in the process, the core concept embodied there can be a good starting point.

The best scenario is when a significant portion of the organization favorably responds to a rallying cry for change. This is often the case once you start the strategic leadership process. Typically, there is a significant degree of alignment when you begin the dialog about the key issues facing the organization. In fact, time and again when asked to identify three key organizational issues that must be addressed, groups working in separate rooms will identify common issues. Often, these are cross-functional groups with very different day-to-day duties, such as may be found between a water meter reader and the head of the electrical department, and yet they always return with significant overlap in their responses. The resulting commonality in responses is often a pleasant surprise to the workshop participants and serves to build the common organizational direction that forms the basis for the rallying cry for change. It also serves to show the power of the process and make it somewhat less intimidating, reflected in comments such as, "Maybe change won't be so bad after all…"

Beyond Staff

To this point, the focus has been on building understanding and buy-in across staff including management and executive staff. There are other key stakeholders who are also vital to the success of the effort—namely the governing body or board. Someone on the governing body may well be the lead Change Agent, or they may have been readily brought into the process early as a strong advocate or co-leader in the change process. Whatever the case, the buy-in and support of the governing body is essential to move the process forward. At the very least, their consent is required.

A reasonable question often surfaces related to the role of external stakeholders, or customers, in the change process. Although customer perspectives are essential—and customer research of some kind is built into this process—they often do not have an active role in the planning process because they are neither well versed in the details of the utility business, nor do they have the time to devote to the effort. If the nature of the change is such that broader stakeholder involvement is important, it is best to define an advisory role and empanel a diverse group of external thought and opinion leaders.

For organizational change to succeed, staff, management and the board must acknowledge the need to address one or more significant internal or external issues confronting the organization. Without the participation of all three groups, change will most likely falter at some point downstream in the process. The combination of active and engaged participation on the part of all three stakeholder groups combines to create a sweet spot, that space where productive and positive change can and will occur. The following diagram illustrates the three key stakeholder groups and the importance of equal and balanced support from each.

Successful Strategic Planning Requires Support from All Three Key Stakeholder Groups

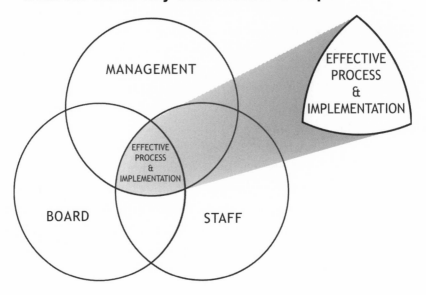

TWO VERY DIFFERENT BOARDS

A large water agency embarked on the development of a strategic plan using The Art of Strategic Leadership *process. As the process was initiated, it became clear that this particular board functions as an operational board, micromanaging management decisions, rather than as a policy board. Even though management and staff passionately endorsed the proposed changes, the process required modification to account for the condition that the agency's board of directors never fully engaged with active, direct involvement. The lesson learned reinforces that the board, management and staff must all be engaged in the process in order to create the "sweet spot" that allows for change to most effectively occur. Although change is taking place at the agency cited here, it is at a significantly slower pace than the management would like and would otherwise be possible with an engaged board.*

By contrast, the board of another water agency seized the opportunity for change and improvement brought on by The Art of Strategic Leadership *process and provided compelling direction and support funding necessary for staff to be successful. In fact, this board was so supportive that they, in effect, functioned as the Change Agent and provided leadership until staff could assimilate and accept the necessary changes. As a result, this organization is addressing some very difficult issues, has gotten its capital program back on track and is implementing its plan in record time.*

Change is successfully realized when everyone in the organization is involved in the change process. Too often change is attempted by an individual or small group. When this occurs, invariably the first to nix a proposed initiative are those not involved in the decision process or a group that feels threatened. This undermines the entire process and must be addressed while in the framework phase of the process for best results.

Language Is Important

Experience has shown time and again that language is important. Significant misunderstandings can result over confusion about common usage of terms. No area of organizational work has suffered more from lack of consistency in the use of language than the various forms of planning. What actually is the difference between vision and mission? Are goals and objectives the same thing? And what are strategies anyway?

In fact, heated arguments often ensue that ultimately boil down to two parties being in "vehement agreement" because they have not agreed on simple semantics. There is always room to argue over the definition of terms, but to put all that to rest, we provide the following definitions to be used throughout this process. We highly recommend that you end the debate and select defined terms you can agree on, and then use them consistently across your organization.

DEFINITIONS
Strategic Direction: Where the organization wants to be in five years.

Strategic Leadership Plan (SLP): A specific, actionable five-year plan that drives the organization toward achieving its Strategic Direction.

Tactical Action Plan (TAP): A one-year work plan describing specifically how the organization will move toward its Strategic Direction, including tasks, budgets, schedule, assignments and accountability.

Vision: What your organization wants to become.

Mission: How your organization will achieve its Vision.

Gap Analysis: A comparison of current and desired future states.

Issue: A problem, concern or challenge that your organization must address.

Goal: How your organization will know when an Issue has been resolved.

Strategy: How an Issue will be resolved.

Tactic: Specific work activity to accomplish a Strategy.

Performance Metric: How progress will be measured.

Sponsor: A "Project Manager" responsible for managing the budget and schedule for an Issue.

Champion: Person with a passion to drive a Strategy forward.

Core Values: Attributes that are fundamental to the way we conduct business.

Core Work Function: A work activity that your organization must perform to "keep the lights on."

Early Wins: Those actions that can be implemented immediately.

Stop-Doing List: Actions that the organization should discontinue or possibly outsource.

Core Planning Team (CPT): A cross-functional team assembled to participate in the planning process.

Senior Management Team (SMT): A team drawn from organizational leadership to act as mentors to those on the CPT; used in larger organizations.

Building Organizational Buy-In

Business schools teach the principle of the Rule of Thirds. In essence, when a new idea is introduced into an organization, the resulting response from staff is predictable. One third of staff will immediately embrace the new idea. Another third will behave like fence sitters and demand more information before passing judgment. And the final third will summarily reject the new idea with little consideration. Management typically focuses its effort on winning over the last third, the group that has rejected the idea, whereas it might better be focusing its effort on the middle third, which typically requires less persuasion to get on board. Once this development occurs, the last third will divide into two. Half will join the majority in support of the idea, and the remaining half, or one-sixth of the entire organization, will steadfastly refuse to willingly participate. They may become toxic, with the unconscious or even conscious objective of killing the idea.

Seeking Endorsement

The hallmark of this process is the powerful concept of organizational endorsement. Endorsement, as featured in *The Art of Strategic Leadership,* addresses the reality of the Rule of Thirds and minimizes the impact of the negative group. By way of definition, endorsement in this process means that an individual or a group may not necessarily agree fully with a decision or outcome, but will find merit with 80 percent of the idea. Furthermore, they will not impede progress, but will help with forward progress by actively providing support. The objective of 100 percent endorsement, in contrast to the Rule of Thirds, is illustrated in the following figure.

Getting from the Rule of Thirds to Endorsement

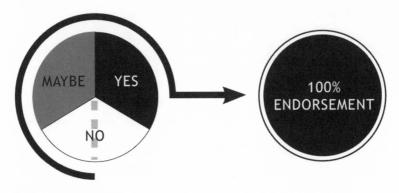

The Art of Strategic Leadership describes how to gain 100 percent endorsement from the entire organization; from field personnel to the boardroom. Is it possible? Numerous case studies can be offered in defense of utilizing an approach that features endorsement. In fact, some time is required to create a culture that embraces change, but in the end the endorsement process is time and money well invested because of the benefits from gaining full endorsement. The Rule of Thirds is largely avoided and no longer applies when the entire organization participates.

Consensus vs. Endorsement

Remember the days of consensus building? The time commitment was enormous and the cost was high. In fact, the need to get virtually every person in an organization to overtly agree before moving forward seems somewhat ludicrous in hindsight. Not only is it overly costly, the consensus-based model is not sustainable without continuing that same level of high energy input. People will change their minds for a variety of reasons—personal, new information, a conversation around the water cooler and so on. As energy is focused on the one-third rejecters, you lose momentum with others who are positively engaged. A true consensus model sets the expectation that each concern be explored and validated. Experience has shown repeatedly that this is not realistic. In fact, each concern cannot be explored and validated; therefore, support for the process predictably falls off at some point in time.

By contrast, endorsement can be achieved and sustained at an acceptably high level without constantly demanding more time and energy. This is because the structure of endorsement is quite different and the organization's set of expectations differ as well. The graphic below illustrates that once endorsement is achieved at an acceptably high level, it continues at that level without significant additional time and energy necessary to sustain it. By contrast, the consensus curve shows that significantly more time, energy and therefore cost are required to reach slightly higher initial agreement in the organization and subsequently that it cannot be sustained with time due to the limitation imposed by the expectation that all concerns must be explored and validated. It is also apparent from the graph that the complete and total agreement central to a consensus approach is not attainable in the first place.

Endorsement Can Be Sustained Over a Longer Time Than Consensus

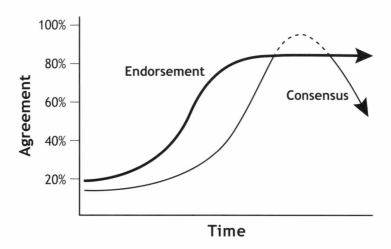

We all know about the Law of Diminishing Returns, which is the tendency for a continuing application of effort or skill toward a particular project or goal to decline in effectiveness after a certain level of result has been achieved. One of the key problems with a consensus-based process is that it ignores the reality of this law and instead seeks to keep at it until that last incremental agreement is reached. The endorsement model is based on applying this law to the advantage of the organization by getting the buy-in required in an efficient amount of time, then allowing the full endorsement to grow as the process progresses. In this way, the process can continue to move forward while others opt to endorse, without stalling each step of the way trying to build consensus. The Law of Diminishing Returns as it applies to the consensus process is displayed in the following graph.

The Law of Diminishing Returns

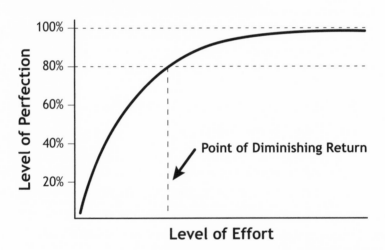

YOU CAN'T CRAFT CONSENSUS

"Been there. Done that. Basically drove us out of business." That's how one frustrated executive responded to an important process that was being framed as designed to build consensus. The group held a higher than

average divergence of opinions—all the more reason to move to a model that features endorsement rather than consensus. The stakes were high—reaching agreement in order to move forward was essential to many of the stakeholders at the table, and for many there was a sense of true urgency related to their growing wastewater treatment needs. Giving everyone an equal voice in impacting direction—which is often how consensus is interpreted—can result in an effort dissolving under the weight of its own misplaced drive for inclusion through consensus. In this case, the intergovernmental entity ultimately dissolved, with key players unable to act in a different way and lead the necessary change.

Creating a Team

When it comes to change, the key to gaining endorsement from 100 percent of the organization is to create an effective team. The components of the team usually consist of a Core Planning Team (CPT), staff and the governing body. An oversight Senior Management Team (SMT) is often used for larger organizations.

The CPT consists of approximately 20 active participants, consisting of the Change Agent, GM/CEO and his or her direct reports, middle managers, and staff-level personnel. The CPT includes opinion leaders, union representatives, and younger members of the organization who are the next generation of leaders. Diverse teams are more effective than homogenous teams. Ideally, the CPT will exhibit diversity in many ways including communication style, gender, age, organizational role, tenure with the organization, creativity, logic, subject matter expertise, educational background, career experiences and a variety of other representative traits, depending on the composition of the organization itself. This diversity is designed not only to offer opportunity to a broad cross section of the organization, but also makes good business sense. Business today is in increasing need of reflecting its customers and other stakeholders; diversity in the CPT is one way to account for this.

It is important to note that since the governing board normally has policy-making responsibilities, its members should not participate on the CPT but are brought in via another part of the process.

Communication Style

One key consideration in naming members to the CPT is to account for communication styles. In order to create an effective team, there must be enough of the various styles represented to create strong dialog and bring both analytical and strategic issues to the fore. There is a variety of models used in the workplace related to understanding personal styles and preferences as well as how they are behaviorally expressed in organizations. In this book, we suggest one such model, although others are valid as well. The point is that the CPT needs to represent a cross section of styles and the process must be facilitated in such a way as to draw upon the perspectives of all. The fact is that each organization is made up of a diverse group of individuals. If the CPT does not reflect this diversity, the viability of the work done and the communication to the organization will be diminished.

In their book *Social Style/Management Style*, Robert and Dorothy Bolton describe the four styles as Driver, Expressive, Analytical and Amiable. As with many such models, the overall population falls into the four quadrants in approximately equal percentages.

The Four Communication Styles

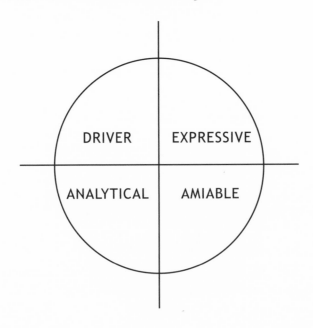

Again, the ideal CPT—and organization for that matter—is populated by a variety of personal styles and communication types. The four communication styles are:

- Driver: Prefers control; highly directive
- Expressive: Prefers dialog; highly emotive
- Amiable: Prefers cooperation; highly conciliatory
- Analytical: Prefers data; highly detailed

The value of having representation from each of these communication styles is the balance that will be achieved from those who bring different perspectives, such as those who are risk takers and those who are risk averse, among other things.

One more note on communication style differences before moving on. The fact is that technical organizations naturally attract those with high analytical skills and rightfully so. The flipside of this is evident when that style is mapped as having introverted, task-oriented and change- or risk-averse communication traits. As shown below, the vast majority of people at infrastructure organizations are introverts with a tendency to undercommunicate; this has been validated in many organizations. An effective strategic leader will be aware of this and learn to compensate as necessary in his or her communication style when relating to others on the staff.

Technical Organizations Tend to Attract Introverts

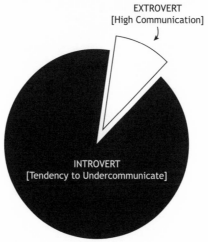

Not only do many who excel at analytical fields not have the innate tendencies toward extroversion and communication that are important for effective leadership, they also receive little if any training in this area while pursuing a rigorous technical degree as illustrated below. *The Art of Strategic Leadership* provides a methodology for those in leadership positions to strengthen communication skills. The tools and techniques provided are a recipe of sorts for the leader to follow that will result in more effective communication both within the CPT and across the organization.

Technical People Typically Have Received Little Communications Training

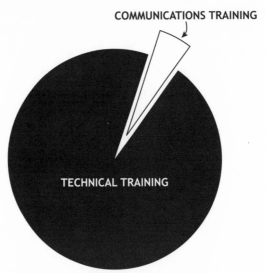

COMMUNICATIONS TRAINING

TECHNICAL TRAINING

DISCOUNTING THE HUMAN ASPECT

A genius by some accounts (including an IQ exam) and a manager by title, one executive that we have worked with refuses to acknowledge the role and insight that such style profiles provide. As a result he is failing—not because he is incapable intellectually. On the contrary, all acknowledge that he is one of the brightest people in the firm. However, his lack of emotional/social intelligence means that he cannot effectively exercise strategic leadership and build a team that is productive and dynamic. Instead, he is constantly fighting unnecessary battles that are easily avoided with some simple understanding of human nature and the individual styles that are brought to the workplace. Bottom line, he is failing as a strategic leader, an absolutely critical aspect of his position in the organization because he discounts the importance of the human, interpersonal aspects of organizational reality, a recipe for failure.

Building and Maintaining Momentum

Creating change requires energy. Increasing energy within a system can be accomplished in a variety of ways, and we have already talked about one—a sense of urgency. The second way to create the positive energy necessary for change is through a focused work effort that builds momentum and enthusiasm through a focused schedule.

The ideal schedule required in *The Art of Strategic Leadership* process calls for CPT members to meet for full-day workshops every two weeks, for a total of approximately ten sessions. The precise number of sessions depends on the scope of the task at hand. Such a schedule represents a significant commitment for each participant, since most have responsibilities that fill a normal eight-hour workday. Although there may be a tendency to modify the schedule, it is vital that the interval between CPT workshops does not exceed three weeks, as focus and momentum is lost, information is forgotten, and inefficiencies begin to derail the process.

Change is often difficult to achieve, especially in those organizations that have weak leadership, strong traditions, collective bargaining agreements, or a history of supporting the status quo. In such organizations, many efforts related to planning, strategic leadership and change management have failed, simply because staff has not been given adequate time to discuss options and understand the impacts of change.

Staff needs to be part of the solution. For these and many other reasons, we have found that frequent CPT workshops are required to successfully implement change, especially if new ideas impact the organization's culture. A worst-case scenario is when management, as a result of short-changing the process, concludes that staff has adopted new ideas, but in reality it has not. Equally serious is when management believes that communicating once with staff on a topic should get the job done and does not acknowledge the amount of commitment required to create lasting organizational change. Such perspectives can create a frustrating and confrontational relationship between management and staff, even to the point of bringing the organization to gridlock conditions.

LACK OF TRUST GRIDLOCK

A large water agency is in gridlock because of a severe lack of trust that exists between all three levels of the organization (between the board and management, and between management and staff). Staff and management are at loggerheads regarding outsourcing of work, and the board is micromanaging management's decisions. A few years ago management prepared a strategic plan, but it failed because staff was not engaged in its development and implementation. The lesson learned is that organizations, large and small, must include everyone in the process, from the boardroom to field personnel, in order for issues to be fully resolved and for the implementation phase to be effective.

In the graphic below, a recommended schedule of meetings for all components of the team within the organization are highlighted.

Recommended Schedule for Strategic Change Process

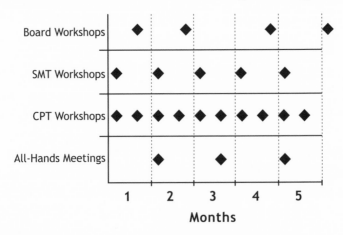

As with all processes, there is room for flexibility and exceptions. If the organization is quite small or if the focus is quite narrow, then the total number of CPT meetings might be reduced and remain effective.

Further, for organizations with a staff count of 400 or more, a Senior Management Team (SMT) should be formed to provide guidance and strategic direction to the CPT. Normally, a large organization will have several executive-level positions. Because the CPT is best limited to approximately 20 staff from across the organization, only a portion of the executive team from a larger organization could participate on the CPT. In order to engage all direct reports under this scenario, an SMT which will preferably include the executive staff would ideally meet prior to every other CPT meeting. For small or medium-sized organizations, the board can provide this important leadership role.

Before Beginning

In most organizations, change is rarely welcomed. On the whole, human nature prefers the status quo. Recall from Chapter 1 that most people and organizations are at least somewhat novophobic.

Even though the CPT consists of the best and brightest minds and opinion leaders in the organization, some will look favorably and some unfavorably toward change. Prior to the first CPT meeting, members of the CPT, SMT and governing board should be conditioned to the need for change, and given an assignment to read *Who Moved My Cheese?* by Spencer Johnson and *Leading Change* by John P. Kotter. Another important reading to frame the process is Jim Collins' *Good to Great*. These books will help readers understand the value and necessity of change and that when done well, change is most definitely not a "flavor of the month" approach or an exercise that occurs every three to five years when conditions require management to be in a reactive mode. These books offer different, but clear statements of why change is necessary and how that change will favorably impact the organization's culture.

The Role of Governing Bodies

Governing bodies play a valuable role in any public sector organization. For this process to work well, board members must be active participants.

Change occurs throughout the organization including at the board level, and will likely fail without at least minimal board involvement. The board is not immune to change—indeed they are part of it. In fact, the final loop in defining Strategic Direction is to make sure that board governance policies align with the direction established. All too often, governance policy either does not even exist or is outdated enough that it lacks alignment with the organizational direction established.

Boards, particularly for public sector organizations, often misunderstand or lack experience in regard to their roles and responsibilities. New board members are usually given no training, so the situation can perpetuate for many years. This can have a negative impact on the organizations they govern both in day-to-day operations and during a planning process.

In general, governing boards are characterized as either policy or operational boards. Operational boards are engaged in the day-to-day business of the organization and spend little time thinking strategically. Some operational boards retain authority to decide purchases of the smallest and most mundane things. Worst-case scenarios are those boards that micromanage and do not empower management. Policy boards, on the other hand, have a clear understanding of their role and the role of the GM/CEO, and focus their time on monitoring GM/CEO performance and the strategic impacts of change on the organization, whether they are from internal or external sources. This book presents the optimal role for boards and how to evolve into this role in Chapter 5.

Appetite for Change

From the outset, the Change Agent must give consideration to and monitor the effects of the organization's appetite for change. If an organization is suffering from chronic issues that are having a serious impact on morale and affecting individual and organizational performance, appropriate corrective action will most likely require significant change across several parts of the organization.

When change is needed, the first reaction from many employees might be, "Change is fine, just as long as it doesn't impact or involve me." If the prognosis requires the setting of a fracture by an orthopedic surgeon, an adhesive bandage won't solve the problem. However, organizational focus on change cannot be so extensive that daily activities grind to a halt. This is another way of saying the organization is unable to reliably fulfill its core business responsibilities (deliver power, water, etc.) because too many staff members are engaged in implementing strategic initiatives or concerned with how the change will impact them personally.

Focus and Forced Prioritization

Again, *The Art of Strategic Leadership* is a pragmatic and practical approach which recognizes and incorporates organizational reality. Accordingly, a key method used to create real change is to focus activities and force prioritization every step of the way. Many processes result in a laundry list of critiques, ideas, directions and activities. This results in dilution of the organization's energy and creates a condition ripe for failure. *The Art of Strategic Leadership*, conversely, only allows a certain number of concepts to go forward during any given cycle, thus greatly increasing the likelihood that the organization will be able to accomplish those items targeted. This is accomplished by embedding an evaluation and prioritization model within each step of the process.

The Art of Strategic Leadership presents a comprehensive change process that produces two basic documents: a Strategic Leadership Plan (SLP) and a Tactical Action Plan (TAP). The SLP presents the key Issues, Strategies, and Goals of the organization with supporting information as may be appropriate, including Vision, Performance Metrics, and so forth. The TAP contains specific actions that must be completed in order to achieve the stated Goals, together with appropriate budgets, schedules, accountability and deliverables. Although there are some elements that this approach shares with traditional strategic planning processes, there are key differences worth noting as highlighted in the following table.

Hallmarks of *The Art of Strategic Leadership*

Issues	Solutions	Benefits
Traditional strategic planning processes often focus significant amounts of time on identifying mission, vision and objectives. Often, these processes fail to recognize the unique culture and specific needs of infrastructure organizations. As a result, the organizational issues the strategic plans seek to address are obscure or not defined at all, and the plans are not an effective tool for solving the organization's problems.	*The Art of Strategic Leadership* has been specifically developed to help infrastructure organizations with implementation of organizational improvements and change. It is an issues-driven process, meaning the entire process is founded on identifying organizational Issues, prioritizing them, and then developing Strategies that solve the Issues.	• Taking the effort to identify succinct organizational issues enhances the organization's ability to develop focused solutions. • Typically, more issues are identified than can realistically be addressed. Prioritizing the issues to the top three or five improves the chances of successful implementation. • The organization is better able to maintain its focus and address the question, "How does this solve the issue?"
Typically, one-third of an organization is comprised of naysayers who find any kind of change difficult. This is often especially true with infrastructure organizations because of their high population of change-averse analytical staff. Most strategic planning processes make the mistake of trying to achieve group consensus on each step of the process as it moves forward. An inordinate amount of time is spent trying to convince an entrenched one-third of the organization. The downside is that the other two-thirds often grow impatient with the lack of progress and lose interest.	*The Art of Strategic Leadership* process is designed to fully involve all levels of the organization in a way that has been proven to achieve endorsement of the change process from 100 percent of staff, senior management and board members. (Endorsement differs from consensus in that it requires a lower threshold of buy-in from the naysayers, such that they agree to not oppose or hinder others from making change happen.)	• Focusing on achieving endorsement, and not consensus, keeps the process from bogging down. The organization stays energized and is able to maintain momentum. • Achieving 100 percent endorsement from all levels of the organization results in the entire organization "owning" the results. Thus, it does not become "management's plan." • Because the documents are owned by the board, senior management and staff, they become part of an organization's culture and management toolkit.

Issues	Solutions	Benefits
It is common to see strategic plans that list far more objectives than can be accomplished within a reasonable period of time. Because the plans fail to account for other time constraints and cost limitations within the organization, they are not implemented; they sit on a bookshelf and become the pride of their authors.	The Strategic Leadership Plan (SLP) provides strategic direction for 3 to 5 years, and includes an annual Tactical Action Plan (TAP) that provides implementation Tactics, including Performance Metrics and accountability, for accomplishment.	All Tactics undertaken during any calendar or fiscal year account for the organization's "appetite for change."
It is common to see strategic plans that are updated on an infrequent basis or when conditions mandate; little is typically done during intervening years.	SLP and TAP are updated annually, providing a rolling 3- to 5-year plan, and are updated prior to the budget planning cycle, providing a means for continuous change.	The SLP and TAP are fluid and dynamic, meaning they are easily amended to reflect changing conditions.

Facilitation

As with most processes that may have an impact on your organization, a key role is that of the process facilitator. Not only should he or she be thoroughly familiar with the change process ultimately adopted, he or she should possess traditional facilitation skills and the following attributes:

- Exercises good listening skills
- Likes working in front of groups
- Knows how to work with the dynamics of a group of people
- Demonstrates ability to adjust direction based on group needs
- Adjusts to new and developing information
- Recognizes that one size or solution doesn't fit all circumstances
- Displays a sensitivity to cultural differences and the need or flexibility
- Understands the role of organizational culture and business process

The Approach

The Art of Strategic Leadership presents a process that has been developed and tested with numerous organizations, large and small, public and private. It is flexible and can be adjusted to meet the specific needs of any organization; however, the complete process generally requires four to five months to complete. It is typically used by entities that recognize the importance of strategy and have existing or emerging leaders who can act as Change Agents. The process is an integrative one and includes the identification of issues and solutions that have significant impact on the Strategic Direction of the organization. The plan is revisited and updated every year as part of the organization's annual budgeting process. The basic principles also apply in other more focused applications such as conflict resolution sessions and focused organizational changes limited to one or two issues.

By design, *The Art of Strategic Leadership* is dynamic and fluid, and produces a fully endorsed plan that will achieve lasting change and positive impact on the organization. In fact, organizations that have embraced *The Art of Strategic Leadership* have incorporated its concepts in their annual business planning and budget cycle, as demonstrated by the following example from a large energy utility.

Incorporating *The Art of Strategic Leadership* into Annual Planning and Budgeting Cycle

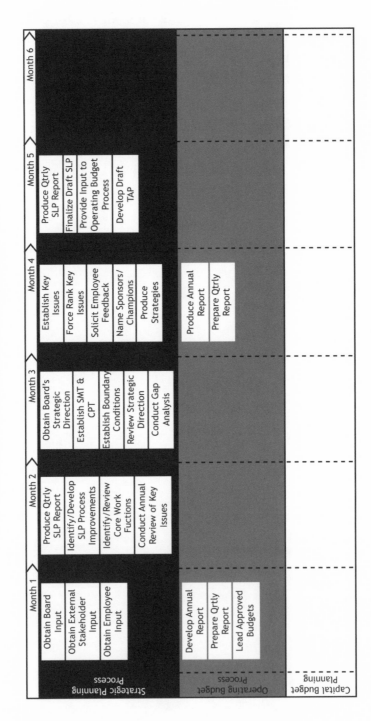

	Month 1	Month 2	Month 3	Month 4	Month 5	Month 6
Strategic Planning Process	Obtain Board Input; Obtain External Stakeholder Input; Obtain Employee Input	Produce Qtrly SLP Report; Identify/Develop SLP Process Improvements; Identify/Review Core Work Fuctions; Conduct Annual Review of Key Issues	Obtain Board's Strategic Direction; Establish SMT & CPT; Establish Boundary Conditions; Review Strategic Direction; Conduct Gap Analysis	Establish Key Issues; Force Rank Key Issues; Solicit Employee Feedback; Name Sponsors/ Champions; Produce Strategies	Produce Qtrly SLP Report; Finalize Draft SLP; Provide Input to Operating Budget Process; Develop Draft TAP	
Operating Budget Process	Develop Annual Report; Prepare Qtrly Report; Lead Approved Budgets			Produce Annual Report; Prepare Qtrly Report		
Capital Budget Planning						

	Month 7	Month 8	Month 9	Month 10	Month 11	Month 12
Strategic Planning Process	Obtain SMT Approval for SLP; Identify Organizational Adjustments; Produce Communications Plan; Finalize TAP	Obtain Board Approval; Publish SLP/TAP; Produce Qtrly SLP Report				Produce Work Orders & Projects
Operating Budget Process	Prepare Payroll/O&M Budget; Distribute Operating Budget Instructions; Prepare Qtrly Report		Conduct Management Hearings	Prepare Qtrly Report	Obtain Budget Committee Approval; Finalize Operating Budget	Obtain Board Operating Budget Approval; Distribute Approved Budget
Capital Budget Planning	Prepare Payroll/Capital Budget	Distribute Capital Budget Instructions	Conduct Management Hearings		Obtain Finance Committee Approval	Obtain Board Capital Budget Approval; Distribute Approved Budget

CPT = Core Planning Team; SMT = Senior Management Team; SLP = Strategic Leadership Plan; TAP = Tactical Action Plan

3

Planning
Tools and Techniques of Strategic Leadership

We have come to the point where the decision has been made and it is time for action. Enough setup and discussion; time to roll up our sleeves and get started! As a strategic leader in the organization, either by title or function, it is clear to you that change is needed, but precisely how does it happen? What comes next? The path from knowing the organization needs change to actually making change happen can seem daunting and full of opportunities to lose track of the initial clarity and direction. This section details the steps of the strategic leadership process and will address common leadership questions such as:

- How do we formulate and get agreement on a compelling direction?
- What is the role of staff and how can we get them engaged?
- Is there a way to get the board engaged and supportive?
- How is this communicated?
- What is the action plan?
- How do we hold the organization accountable?
- How do we know if we are on track?

Soon the steps will be clear for getting from point A (understanding and continually promoting the need for a culture of change) to Point B (clearly defining and prioritizing the issues or problems to solve) and to Point C (taking the appropriate action steps to implement, monitor and sustain change). The process is not rocket science. All its elements have been around since the beginning of management consulting. There are no new theoretical ideas presented, but new insight to their application has been developed as experience has necessitated refinement. Development of *The Art of Strategic Leadership* has been guided by simplicity. All employees, regardless of background, can participate in and contribute to the process.

To initiate action, the Change Agent now needs to request that the Senior Management Team (SMT) and board of directors endorse a formal call for organizational change. The GM/CEO, SMT and board must anticipate the question "Why are we doing this?" from Core Planning Team (CPT) members, staff and/or union representatives. The response must be uniform and it must contain a sense of urgency. The board or SMT needs to provide a set of instructions for the CPT by defining the Strategic Direction of the organization. In other words, the critical success factors that the Strategic Leadership Plan (SLP) will be measured against need to be defined. Once this is done, the Change Agent will identify members of the CPT and name a process facilitator, and then present an overview of the change process to the entire organization via an all-hands meeting or formal written communiqué. The senior management call to change and organizational guidance will be reviewed and refined by the CPT and SMT in the initial workshops.

The rest of this chapter presents the objectives and agendas for the recommended total of ten CPT workshops. Each workshop will be six to seven hours long, and the entire process will span four to five months. Although each workshop agenda is presented in a project schedule format, the real world has proven time and again that it often does not operate as planned. This process is not rigid. In fact, it is essential that a change process such as this reflects the dynamics of the organization and the group. The Change Agent and the facilitator need to make sure the entire group is brought along. It takes a good deal of finesse to move an organization toward the change that it needs. Explanations are offered only for some of the agenda items noted, as many are self-explanatory. Before beginning the first CPT workshop, the CPT, SMT and board members should have read the books recommended in Chapter 1. Since each CPT workshop consumes roughly six to seven hours of time, careful planning must occur to minimize work disruptions and conflicts. The facilitator should establish the schedule dates for all the workshops prior to the first meeting so that participants can get all the meetings onto their calendars. A scribe should be appointed to document meeting discussions.

The following flow diagram shows the progression through the strategic leadership process. Depending on the varying needs for each organization, the steps may not be precisely in the order shown, and some may receive more attention than others. In fact, the ability to be responsive to the organizational needs "on the fly" is essential to a successful process and outcome. The entire process is simple, but not easy. It clearly requires an ability to adjust to the organization's needs as they become better clarified during the process.

The Steps in the Strategic Leadership Process

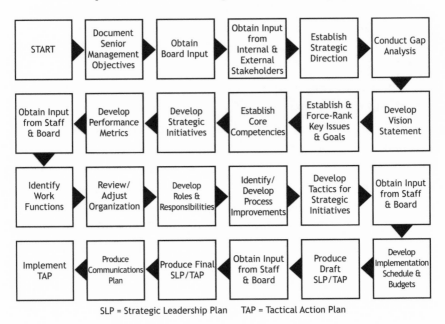

SLP = Strategic Leadership Plan   TAP = Tactical Action Plan

While implementing the process, the Change Agent needs to understand the need for flexibility and at the same time needs to trust the process. The understanding of the organization's fitness evolves and becomes clearer as a part of the process itself; therefore, the process—and the participants including strategic leaders, CPT members and facilitator—must be flexible and agile.

STUMBLING BLOCK

One of the stumbling blocks organizations often confront while implementing The Art of Strategic Leadership *relates to organizational structure. In several instances, it is clear that the organization was not designed to respond to the Capital Improvement Program that was necessary for continued high quality service to customers. By contrast, in one instance, the utility had developed a clear organizational mission through a thorough process a few years earlier and determined that it was still applicable and meaningful to the organization. So, to respond to this organizational reality, the planning team spent more time on the possible organizational solutions with minimal time spent refreshing the mission/vision as that was still valid. Depending on the needs of the organization, the process flexes to create a path forward.*

Workshop #1: Getting Started
"Why are we here anyway?"
Workshop Objective: Assemble the team and launch the process.

At the outset, the GM/CEO should plan to make some opening remarks at the first workshop to underscore the importance of the activity to the organization and to the members of the CPT. The GM/CEO's remarks are best if they are brief and sincere and if they clearly state the sense of urgency. They should leave no doubt in any-one's mind that the effort is essential and is important to the board and to the organization. The information covered should include items such as:

- Summarize why change is needed: "Over the next five years 30 percent of our staff will be retiring."
- Feature a sense of urgency: "If we don't act now, the Council will reconsider our structure to ensure delivery of critical services."
- Underscore the importance of the role of the CPT members: "The organization is looking to all of you who were selected as CPT members to identify and contribute to positive changes needed to move the organization forward."

WORKSHOP #1 AGENDA:

1. Welcome, GM/CEO opening remarks and review agenda
2. Introduce the process facilitator
3. Conduct book review
4. Discuss change process, schedule and deliverables
5. Discuss roles/responsibilities of CPT, SMT, staff, and board
6. Discuss role/responsibility of GM/CEO

7. Review CPT ground rules and principle of endorsement
8. Discuss call to action and critical success factors
9. Conduct gap analysis
10. Establish draft Issues

The cornerstone of *The Art of Strategic Leadership* is a clear, succinct identification of the critical Issues that are driving the need for change within the organization. In addition, the concept must be driven home that because the organization is very busy it will be necessary throughout the process to limit the amount the organization is willing and able to tackle. Accordingly, Issues must be identified and then prioritized down to a manageable few; typically no more than five Issues will be addressed at any given time. Smaller organizations may want to take on no more than three (or fewer) Issues at a time, depending on their appetite for change.

Much of the background and context for the planning effort that is presented during Workshop #1 is covered in the previous chapters. In addition, it is important to reinforce the leadership theme as one of the CPT selection criteria, thus building each member's view of themselves in this regard. Depending on the team, sometimes it is beneficial to embed a mini-workshop on leadership itself, using a leadership training video or other such tool for discussion.

During Workshop #1, it is also important to alert the CPT members to the fact that planning is hard work. People often come to serve on such teams without preparation and expect an easy day. Effective planning workshops require a lot of thinking; as one participant remarked after a day-long session developing Tactical Action Plans, "This is hard work; my brain hurts!" Moreover, the planning sessions are the easy part; implementation requires an even higher degree of focus and accountability. During the first workshop, the CPT needs to understand the work ahead of them and be prepared to actively engage. Their brains indeed will hurt at the end of the day!

Recurring Responsibilities

There are several items that occur between each workshop. Such items are important to the effectiveness of the process and include documenting the output of each session and communicating with staff to build buy-in and endorsement.

After each workshop, the output of that session is documented in thorough meeting notes. This step is essential as it forms the basis of the group's memory and documents decisions and direction as the process moves forward. It allows for the "dialog—draft—revisit—decide" iterative cycle that builds to a clear direction. Without thorough and clear documentation, time and momentum are lost and trust in the process can erode.

Based on the output summarized in the workshop notes, the CPT members have a standing—and vital—homework assignment. As staff that has been identified as leaders, CPT members are best positioned to initiate the necessary organizational dialog to build endorsement across the organization. Therefore, each CPT member will be expected to take the work from each session, discuss it with other staff, gather feedback, and bring the feedback to the next workshop. This is an ongoing responsibility of every CPT member and is essential to gaining the endorsement needed to create a broadly accepted plan that will be implemented.

In addition, after each CPT workshop the facilitator, Change Agent and GM/CEO should debrief and recalibrate direction as necessary. Recall that the Change Agent may or may not be the GM/CEO. If not, then both must be present and engaged in the discussion that leads to process adjustments. The express purpose of the debrief sessions is to make sure that the progress aligns with GM/CEO, Change Agent and board goals.

During the first workshop it is important that the facilitator read the crowd and be particularly observant of body language and of behavior of the group and individuals. Some individuals will likely be outspoken, some quiet, and some openly antagonistic. The facilitator may see signs of camps forming; these often align with organization silos (e.g., operations vs. engineering or water vs. electric). It is helpful to bring these observations up during the debrief sessions because the facilitator can often gain additional information about the observed behaviors that will be useful in subsequent workshops as the facilitator works to help the CPT become a high-performing team.

Gap Analysis

Opening early in the process with a gap analysis can help CPT members get their brains in alignment to think about Issues, not solutions. At this point, the CPT should break into smaller groups, usually about three or four equal-size groups. Depending on organizational dynamics, allowing the CPT to self-organize may be appropriate; in other cases assigning participants to sub-groups is more effective. In any case, it is perfectly acceptable for staff from the same division or work unit to sit together at first, as they are more apt to participate if they are sitting with their peer group. Over the course of the ten workshops, you would expect to see the need to sit with the home workgroup diminish as the CPT becomes its own team. Normally, 30 to 45 minutes should be allocated for the breakout sessions; this depends entirely on the amount of content to be covered and the pace of the CPT members. Each work session is followed by group reports, further CPT discussion, clarification and agreement.

The objective of the gap analysis is simple; each group should be assigned the task of identifying existing conditions within the organization and then identifying the corollary desired future conditions. Each group then reports out to the CPT as a whole. The CPT will then act as a team to sort, combine and compile its composite gap analysis. The gap analysis is the basic building block for later development of Issue statements.

Throughout the process organizational and individual leadership training also is occurring by design. The process helps CPT members learn how to facilitate, present, take ownership, make their voice heard, listen to others and step up to a new level of leadership. This is built into the structure of the process itself and can be a powerful part of participating in such a process.

Issues Drive the Process

Describing Issues accurately will help the process now and farther down the line. A proven technique for describing an Issue is to require the CPT to develop short sentences that contain one of the following words: *must, needs,* or *should.* The sentence should be no more than six to eight words long. For example, "Workforce efficiencies must be improved" is a well-phrased Issue statement. It is clear and strong, it features a sense of urgency, and it is brief enough that staff can be expected to retain and recall it. By contrast the following statement is neither clear and strong, nor memorable, "Due to the nature of the business environment today, the Department will seek to improve workforce efficiencies."

Early in the process, some CPT members may protest that this approach for the structure of the Issue statements is unnecessarily rigid. What then is the purpose of structuring Issue statements using one of these three words? The answer is that each of these words answers the question, "Why?" By asking *why* several times, a skilled facilitator is able to help the CPT drill down to the fundamental problem or Issue. For example, the CPT for one client organization initially identified as an Issue, "We need to implement a maintenance management software system." The facilitator responded, "That sounds like a great idea, but *why* is this software system needed?" This line of questioning ultimately revealed the real Issue, which was that workforce efficiencies in multiple areas of the organization were lacking (not only in the Maintenance Division) and were in need of significant improvement. When it was pointed out that software improvements might be merely one of many ways to improve efficiency, the CPT agreed that the real Issue needing to be solved could best be described as, "Workplace efficiencies must be improved."

Using the result of the gap analysis as a starting point, there is no limit to the number of initial Issues the CPT can identify. Once all groups have reported, the facilitator, working with the entire CPT, should eliminate duplicates and combine similar ideas. Finally, if there are more than five to seven Issues, they all need to be force-ranked in terms of importance to the CPT and for alignment with the Strategic Direction established by the board or SMT. Although this may appear simple, this exercise of forcing a group to state Issues in the above format, combined with the need to limit the number of Issues going forward, contains embedded organizational change concepts that are quite powerful. By forcing the statements into the essential *must/needs/should* format and limiting the overall count, the CPT has thus distilled a wide assortment of concerns that are swirling about any organization to the most urgent, most time-critical Issues in an efficient and condensed process.

Method to the Madness

Although groups sometimes balk at the prescriptive structure of Issue statements, be assured that there is a method to the madness. In fact, once a team develops Issue statements in the imperative *must/needs/should* structure, their power becomes clear. Instead of unclear statements that are confused as to intent, Issue statements in this format create a sense of urgency and built-in prioritization. Of the many Issues that may be developed during the process, the top three or five identified are clearly those that the organization must address first. This essential element—clearly identifying and stating the Issues—drives the remainder of the strategic leadership process and starts to queue up effective implementation from the outset.

Recall that one of the primary complaints about organizational change processes is that staff feels that, in reality, nothing ever changes. By forcing clarity and prioritization, the organization defines the key leverage points for effective change and creates a focused and actionable plan from the outset of the process.

As noted earlier, the Strategic Leadership Plan (SLP) and Tactical Action Plan (TAP) are updated annually. Thus, if your organization's appetite for change is limited to solving five Issues during the first year and not, for example, the nine initially identified by the CPT, then the remaining four will be documented and will roll over to subsequent years for consideration, along with potential new Issues. Issues development can be done at any time, with any working team.

Workshop #2: Building the Foundation for Change
"Where are we going?"
Workshop Objective: Start to form a common direction.

WORKSHOP #2 AGENDA:

1. Review agenda
2. Review meeting notes from CPT Workshop #1

3. Discuss staff input gained during endorsement process
4. Discuss external stakeholder input
5. Conduct communication style profile analysis of CPT members
6. Draft Vision statement
7. Modify, edit and force-rank Issues
8. Endorse draft Issue and Vision statements
9. Prepare for SMT, board, and all-hands meetings

The first and second CPT workshops have two simple objectives: to form a functioning planning team and to establish the key Issues confronting the organization. Starting with a strong foundation for the teamwork to follow is an important step.

Given the opportunity, a roomful of engineers or other technically oriented people will typically gravitate quickly toward finding a solution, often without fully identifying the Issues they are attempting to solve! Recall that processing change takes time and rushing to solutions—as comfortable as that is, particularly for analytical types—is counterproductive.

The Importance of Communication Styles

Building an effective team can be greatly helped when each CPT member understands his or her personal communication style and those of the other CPT members. Chapter 2 contains a discussion of communication styles. We strongly recommend that your CPT team members go through an exercise in which you conduct an inventory of your own communication styles.

The purpose of surveying and discussing communication style among the CPT is threefold:

1. Knowledge of the CPT composition is helpful to the facilitator in understanding styles which may be over- or underrepresented. For example, a roomful of staff with "amiable" or "analytical" styles will find it difficult to make even small changes.
2. The Change Agent or facilitator can more readily recognize a team or individual behavior that may seem counterproductive but is in fact simply expression of style.

3. The group dialog and understanding developed through this process will improve the functioning and productivity of the team.

For the most part, people are not so simple that they fit entirely into one of the four communication styles discussed in Chapter 2, although that sometimes does happen. A quick note: if one or more CPT members scores very high as a "driver," pay special attention to team dynamics as this will likely have an impact on both the process and outcome, which must be managed.

Stakeholder Input

Strategic leadership planning is often best done in the context of understanding the external market environment, which includes stakeholder perspectives, customer perceptions and political realities. Although statistically valid market research forms an optimal foundation for planning, sometimes this does not occur. If such research is not available, or is not possible to conduct, a sampling of stakeholder perspectives is a useful way to ground the process. This consists of identifying a cross section of stakeholders and conducting one-on-one interviews to ask some very basic, open-ended questions regarding the utility:

- What is going well?
- What needs to be improved?
- What three things would you change if you could?

The point here is to engage in dialog and understand perspectives on the organization and its performance from an external point of view.

Discussing stakeholder input can occur during the first or second CPT workshop, but is best done early in the process. This timing enables the CPT to validate its early direction as it is developed with external perspectives in mind. Typically, the feedback received from stakeholders contains few surprises and, although not always flattering, it serves to orient the CPT in reality and underscore some of its key challenges.

As with many elements of the planning process, the team is looking for alignment between its perspectives—first captured in gap analysis and subsequently in Issue statements—and those of the external environment. Incorporating stakeholder perspectives also serves to drive the organization toward an external focus, an element often lacking or at least in need of reinforcement in many infrastructure organizations.

Dynamics of the Core Planning Team

Once the Issues are drafted and calibrated against the board's Strategic Direction and critical success factors, and input has been received from external stakeholders, the CPT can proceed with the next agenda item. Before this action is taken, a few words are offered regarding the CPT dynamics and chemistry. As noted earlier, the CPT should consist of the organization's best and most talented people. Even so, there may be CPT members who hold the belief, "Change is fine, just as long as it doesn't affect or involve me." There may even be one or two who attempt to stop or derail the process. Invariably, there are parties with this attitude in every organization and they can often be found in titled managerial roles.

The CPT must respond to these challenges without seeming defensive or overreacting. The following ideas may help mitigate such situations:

- Challenge all CPT members to passionately come to each meeting with outside-the-box ideas, and urge them to be bold.
- Require honesty in CPT workshops and reinforce such behavior.
- Employ the parking lot technique, in which comments that are distractions are acknowledged, documented and then dealt with off-line.
- Regularly meet one-on-one with those who are a distraction and are resisting forward progress to resolve questions and concerns, either during breaks or outside of CPT workshops.

Vision Statement

Depending on circumstances a Vision statement can be drafted by the CPT, SMT, or board. For example, if members of the CPT are struggling with some aspect of change, the facilitator could turn to the

SMT to draft the Vision statement. If the board's desire for change is not shared by staff, including the SMT, then the board could draft the Vision statement. Vision helps drive the change process and defines where the organization should be at the end of a defined period, which normally is at least five years out.

The task of developing a Vision can be difficult and demanding. And it should be, especially if your organization is a private sector company burdened with stagnant growth, or a public sector agency that is on the verge of takeover by private companies. A well-stated Vision requires the ability to see the long term and create a compelling picture in somewhat simple terms. It can start in a longer and more narrative form, but should then be shortened for ease of recall.

One of the best examples of Vision can be drawn from recent history. In the late 1950s, the United States and the Soviet Union were vying for world leadership; this was played out in many arenas, one being science and technology. When John F. Kennedy became president he drove a clear stake in the ground with a Vision that the United States would be the world leader in science and technology. That was a lofty Vision given that World War II had ended less than two decades earlier and clear leadership was still emerging. This Vision was further clarified by an associated Mission statement which created a dynamic—and actionable—pair.

The structure of the Vision statement is quite simple. It should be one sentence long. No bullets or run-on sentences are permitted. Someone should be able to read the statement in one breath without hyperventilating. Ideally, it contains a quantifiable number (date, percentage, dollar amount, etc.) and is consistent with the Strategic Direction developed by the board or SMT. Given the following instructions, breakout groups will produce the best results while creating healthy competition:

"Visualize your breakout group in a large green pasture (representing, for example, the marketplace). Your task is to drive a stake into the ground at some distant location in the pasture. The location of the stake is where your organization must be in five to ten years in order to satisfy the Strategic Direction developed by the board or SMT. The description of that 'stake in the ground' represents the Vision statement."

Mission Statement

A Mission statement describes *how* your organization will achieve its Vision. It gives concrete, definite form to the somewhat lofty and intangible Vision. Using the John F. Kennedy example, then, the Mission was clearly stated: "I believe that this nation should commit itself to achieving the goal, before this decade is out, of landing a man on the moon and returning him safely to the earth."[1] Thus, the Mission describes *how* the United States became the world leader in science and technology. Since most organizations become confused with Vision and Mission statements, the process contained in this book retains the Vision statement, but removes the Mission statement simply to eliminate unnecessary debate and confusion. However, organizations that have the ability to develop both can realize a powerful pairing, just as the nation did under President Kennedy's direction. For the purposes of this more streamlined process, the Mission is described by the Goals, Strategies, and Tactics that will be developed later in the process.

Testing the Water

Once the key organizational Issues and Vision statement have been drafted, which should occur during the first and second CPT workshops, it is time to test the water! The change process presented in this book promotes the concept that ultimately 100 percent of employees, from the field to the boardroom, will endorse the Strategic Leadership Plan. The only way this can occur is if members of the CPT regularly submit draft information to those not participating in the workshops and request input from them. The first stop should be the SMT and board.

The SMT and board must contribute to the process, or the results will quickly become meaningless. Why is this so? Quite simply: The power of the purse strings. If the SMT and board have not participated in the process or have not bought into the solution, one or both can sabotage the implementation phase through their power over the budget. Given the opportunity, the SMT and board can provide the CPT with valuable insight and provide strategic direction. The Change Agent must keep them informed and engaged.

---

[1] Special Message to the Congress on Urgent National Needs, 5/22/61.

The response staff provides is also important. Ideally, all employees will meet in small groups with one or more CPT member sometime between each CPT workshop. Each meeting should take approximately 30 to 60 minutes. A proposed agenda is provided for the employee meeting to be held between CPT Workshops #2 and #3. Agendas for other employee meetings would follow a similar format of updating and soliciting feedback.

EMPLOYEE MEETING AGENDA

1. Welcome and overview of the planning process
2. ntroduction of the draft Issues and Vision statement
3. Employee input and comment (provide at least 20 minutes for this activity)
4. Explanation of how subsequent information will be summarized and the process to get feedback from staff

Alternatively, an all-hands meeting can be held to accomplish the same purpose as multiple, smaller meetings. Prior to the meetings, handouts should be produced that clearly present the information being discussed. It is very important that the meeting facilitator (a CPT member) exercise good listening skills. All employee comments should be accurately documented, and the facilitator should concentrate on not behaving defensively if staff criticizes the information developed by the CPT. Staff will be more likely to support ideas if they are given a chance to participate and their input is appropriately documented.

Note that it is important to adjust employee expectations regarding the purpose of these meetings and their feedback. Due to the former consensus-based processes many are familiar with, some employees hold the mistaken notion that all ideas are incorporated. This is not the case. All ideas are respected and will be discussed during the next CPT session, but they may or may not be incorporated into the direction. The CPT is a decision-making body that can take input from others, but ultimately makes the necessary judgments and decisions necessary to craft the plan.

Workshop #3: Developing Draft Strategies
"How are we going to solve the Issues?"
Workshop Objective: Validate and endorse/confirm direction.

WORKSHOP #3 AGENDA:

1. Review agenda
2. Review meeting notes from CPT Workshop #2
3. Discuss input received from board, SMT, and staff
4. Modify and edit Issues
5. Modify Vision statements
6. Review and endorse Issues
7. Endorse Vision statements
8. Develop draft Strategies

Accurately Crafting Issue Statements

Prior to developing any strategies, the CPT should recognize the importance placed on crafting, as accurately as possible, the Issue statements in their final form. Issues were developed and have been discussed throughout the organization, so now it is time to finalize and move forward. Prior to endorsing the Issues as final, adequate time should be taken to review available information, especially input received from the board, staff, management and external stakeholders. The CPT may then summarize comments received and distribute the summary to staff. This is a real winner, because staff will say, "Finally! They are listening."

The CPT is encouraged not to wordsmith the Issue statements at this stage, but rather to question, challenge and probe to ensure that any bias or novophobia has been removed from the process. Again, the organization's appetite for change should be carefully evaluated to ensure that staff can still perform their core work functions without disruption to customers. Methods for creating time so that staff can work on implementation are discussed later in this book. The CPT may have its creative juices flowing at this point, and may generate an extensive list of Issues they feel they want to tackle.

Although the creative energy of the CPT is positive, most organizations can undertake no more than five Issues at a time. Large organizations might manage up to seven, and smaller ones perhaps three. The multiplying effect and rationale for keeping the number of Issues limited is illustrated by the following example. Given five Issues, each Issue might have as many as five Strategies, and each Strategy might have five Tactics with associated specific Task items. Doing the arithmetic results in 125 discrete activities that ultimately have to be assigned, budgeted and accounted for. Thus, the ability to overwhelm an organization to the point of no action becomes clear.

This reinforces the importance of prioritization, one of the hallmarks of the process. The goal is to constantly define and prioritize the possible actions to a list that represents the organization's highest priorities and makes optimal use of the next dollar spent. Throughout the process, a reality check is useful in terms of honestly assessing what your organization can accomplish from the standpoint of budget and staff availability and overall appetite for change. If your organization needs to prioritize further, then be sure to do so. Remember, a Strategic Leadership Plan that is not implemented—resulting in yet another piece of evidence that nothing changes—is largely a waste of time and money. Other techniques to drive toward effective implementation are included in Chapter 4.

The CPT must limit the number of Issues it tackles in order to prevent staff meltdown and implementation challenges later in the process. Remember, since the SLP and TAP are updated annually, Issues that do not make the initial cut will roll over to subsequent years for consideration. At this stage of the process, there is no room for egos or pet rocks. How important are Issue statements? The change process revolves around the accuracy of the Issue statements. If the Issues are correctly identified they will resonate with the entire organization. The CPT must rise to the occasion and demonstrate courage in creating a change environment. Issues spearhead change. It is absolutely essential not to rush this step of the process.

Examples of some well-crafted Issue statements are:

- Department must become more efficient.
- Relationships with external stakeholders must be improved.
- A safety culture must be developed.
- Department morale must be improved.
- A strong and qualified workforce must be attracted and retained.

Strategies and Tactics

Strategies

Strategy development is normally the highlight of the change process, as engineers and technical staff often enjoy identifying solutions. While the initial steps of a planning process appeal to people with more intuitive styles, the work related to developing Strategies and Tactics appeals to the more technical and analytical people. This also underscores the importance of having a diverse group engaged in plan development so that the end product—the Strategic Leadership Plan—is strong from start to finish.

Prior to further CPT work in breakout groups, the team needs to understand the difference between Strategies and Tactics. In a nutshell, a set of Strategies, when accomplished, will resolve an associated Issue. Similarly, completion of a set of Tactics addresses an associated Strategy.

Strategies are clearly stated solutions that solve Issues. Similar to the logic behind the *must/needs/should* structure for the Issue statements, there is an optimal sentence structure for Strategies as well. This structure is summarized as: Feature-Verb-Benefit. This structure frames the thinking more specifically than Issues, but more broadly than the simplicity required for Tactics. Some example Strategies are:

- Outsourcing routine activities enables staff to focus on mission-critical services.
- Heightened focus on external communications improves stakeholder relationships.
- Employee-driven safety program develops safety-minded culture.
- Consistent application of rules and policies improves employee trust.
- Career guidance and training improves employee retention.

Tactics

Tactics are individual action items that, when accomplished, complete a Strategy. For simplicity, and to distinguish them from Strategies, each Tactic begins with an action verb (for example, *maintain, produce, develop*), and should be limited to six to eight words. Examples of Tactics that address a Strategy are:

- Identify non-critical competencies for outsourcing.
- Create department-wide speakers bureau.
- Create employee safety committee.
- Implement supervisor training program.
- Create and fund career guidance counselor position.

The Issues-Strategies-Tactics Set

We have now developed a nested set of Issues, Strategies and Tactics. The following diagram presents such a nested set and provides an overview of how the items dovetail and create increasingly specific statements that add up to address organizational Issues.

The Issue-Strategies-Tactics Set

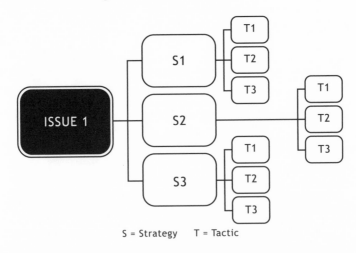

S = Strategy   T = Tactic

Each breakout group should be encouraged to spend 30 to 45 minutes brainstorming Strategies for an assigned Issue. At this point, every idea is a good idea! As the breakout groups develop Strategies for each of the Issues they will move from brainstorming to prioritizing and will ultimately develop a list of seven to ten Strategy statements. After the brainstorming and prioritization phase in the breakout groups, the final step is to frame each Strategy in the Feature-Verb-Benefit structure.

The CPT is then re-engaged as a whole to review, comment, critique and debate the list of Strategies, narrowing them down to no more than three to five potential Strategies to take forward. Again, to manage the scale of work being queued up by the planning process, there is a limit on the number of Strategies for each Issue—no more than five.

Workshop #4: Refining Strategies and Identifying Quantifiable Goals

"Finally, things are starting to make sense."
Workshop Objective: Filling in the details.

WORKSHOP #4 AGENDA:

1. Review agenda
2. Review meeting notes from CPT Workshop #3
3. Discuss staff input gained during endorsement process
4. Discuss Roles/Responsibilities of Issue Sponsors and Strategy Champions
5. Review and modify draft Strategies
6. Develop draft Goals
7. Endorse Goals and Strategies
8. Draft Core Value statements
9. Prepare for SMT, board, and all-hands meetings

Sponsors and Champions

The process is gaining momentum. Things are finally starting to make sense. By now, the CPT should have settled into the process and should have formed a high-performing team. Individual members should be detecting the need to step up to the plate and provide leadership during the implementation phase, which will be discussed later.

As stated at the outset, a secondary benefit of the entire planning process is that it identifies and cultivates leadership. As such, executives on the CPT will likely note which of the CPT members are stepping up into a higher level of their own personal leadership.

At this point in the process, it is becoming increasingly clear that being on the CPT is hard work. Also, the discomfort or "squirm factor" associated with making a personal commitment should be building among CPT members! This bears repeating: planning is hard work, and the real work starts after the plan is adopted and implementation starts.

Eventually, the process requires naming an individual Sponsor for each Issue, as well as a Champion for each Strategy. These Sponsors and Champions are the leaders of the plan implementation team and are responsible for getting their Issues addressed. Toward this end, the Sponsors and Champions must be vested with the appropriate responsibility, accountability and authority to accomplish the plan. During development of TAPs and Task Plans, others across the organization will be drawn into the process and will become an essential part of implementation.

Typically, the vast majority of Sponsors and Champions are also CPT members as they have the more complete understanding and context for the plan and should be well equipped to lead implementation. Age and seniority should not be selection criteria. Passion for change and interest in the subject matter should be winning attributes. At this stage of the process, the facilitator should provide a brief job description for Issue Sponsors, which includes the following:

- Prepare and manage a work plan for all Tactics including tasks, budget and schedule
- Assemble an internal team to help complete assignments; all employees are candidates
- Provide ongoing leadership to the implementation team and ensure that the necessary work is being done

- Remove obstacles to implementation using the endorsed and adopted Strategic Leadership Plan as the driving force
- Monitor progress and report to executive and plan leadership

Core Values

Most organizations have developed a set of Core Values. However, there are those who have not yet accomplished this powerfully effective step in the process. Values are the pathway to being able to understand and discuss—even change—organizational culture. As such, it is an extremely important element. No matter what else leaders try to accomplish, culture always wins, so paying attention here yields noticeable benefits.

The CPT needs to review, or create for the first time, Core Values of the organization to ensure they are consistent with and responsive to the identified Issue statements. For example, if your organization is struggling with timesheet irregularities, then the CPT might consider strengthening or adding Core Values that relate to honesty and integrity. Other Core Values might include respect, innovation and balance to name only a few of the possible Core Values an organization can express and build into behavioral expectations. Accountability is a value that many organizations struggle with, so articulating that as a Core Value is often an essential part of cultural change.

Values definition and development falls into the realm of simple but not easy. It can be simple to come up with the words that most agree on; words such as "integrity" and "honesty" come to mind. But how thorough was the evaluation that led to those words? What do those words mean? How do you translate those words into common, organization-wide understanding?

In order to address this potential gap—we all can agree on the *words* that state our Core Values, but remain confused about what those words actually mean—it has proved powerful to develop a Values-Attributes-Behaviors set as illustrated by the following plan excerpt:

Example Values-Attributes-Behaviors Set

Core Value	Related Attribute	Behavior or Result
Integrity	Honesty	Full disclosure (even about failures); clear communication
	Trustworthiness	Keep commitments; follow through
	Clear Standards	Clearly state behaviors (positive and negative) and consequences
	Responsibility	Use information to address, not manipulate, issues
	Dependability	Step up to the plate and own issues
	Fair and Equal Treatment	Encourage trust among employees, management and public
Leadership/Teamwork	Accountability	Make tough decisions
	Support	Respect and support each other's needs and goals
	Cooperation	Promote a supportive learning environment
	Communication	Promote a feeling of inclusion for all personnel
Excellence	Public Trust	Insist on high-quality work, timeliness, and cost-consciousness
	Commitment	Commitment to high performance
	Continuing Education	Training of employees to ensure improvement of job skills to meet demands

For an even more in-depth and useful treatment of values, several diagnostic instruments are available that form a thorough organization-wide understanding of the topic. These instruments allow you to assess individual values, current organization-wide values and desired organization-wide values in the context of a validated model. This allows an organization to understand alignment and gaps so that key leverage points for change can be identified. A thorough assessment of organization-wide values can be a powerful element of organizational change, but is beyond the scope of this book.

Goal Statements

Goal statements help define when the organization knows it has arrived. They need to provide a clear and concise way to measure when an Issue has been resolved. Goal statements should contain a quantifiable number (date, percentage, dollar amount, etc.). This provides definitive direction regarding when it is time to stop and move on to another Issue. In addition, defined Performance Metrics are an important tool used by the board and senior management to track progress and ensure accountability for results. Once again, breakout groups provide more opportunities for everyone to participate and then loop back with the entire CPT for review, discussion and validation.

Examples of well-expressed Goal statements are provided below:

- By December 2008, a process to continually improve stakeholder involvement will be established and functioning.
- Department will achieve capital project accomplishment rate of 80 percent by December 2008.
- Department will adopt standards that establish accountability and measure quality, productivity and responsiveness by June 2009.

During CPT Workshop #3, the CPT modified Issue and Vision statements in response to input received from the SMT, board and staff. Draft Goals, Values, and Strategies are now documented.

Once again, at the conclusion of CPT Workshop #4, the CPT should endorse the results before presenting this information to the SMT, board and staff. If one or more CPT members are struggling with any aspect of the above-referenced information, everyone must make an effort to understand the concerns and, if necessary, forge a compromise that produces a win-win scenario. At this stage of the process, well managed group dynamics and an effective team will be instrumental in gaining endorsement, without sacrificing quality.

As always, after each CPT workshop, the members are obligated to communicate with staff across the organization to gain endorsement, as discussed previously.

Workshop #5: Putting the Pieces Together

"Wow, there is no way we are going to get all of this done!"
Workshop Objective: Adjust and polish key elements of the plan.

WORKSHOP #5 AGENDA:

1. Review agenda

2. Review meeting notes from CPT Workshop #4
3. Discuss input received from board, SMT, and staff
4. Modify/edit Issues, Goals, Strategies, Vision and Values
5. Review appetite for change
6. Develop draft core work functions and core competencies
7. Conduct gap analysis of current organization chart
8. Develop draft Stop-Doing List

CPT Workshop #5 provides one last opportunity for the CPT to adjust and polish key elements of the Strategic Leadership Plan before beginning the implementation phase and development of a Tactical Action Plan. The entire Strategic Planning model, starting with Issues definition through to the SLP and TAP, is fluid and dynamic. This is necessary to respond to the rapidly changing world we all operate in. For example, following the attacks of 9/11, issues confronting both public and private organizations changed overnight. Security issues rose quickly to the highest priority level. The process adapts well to such changing conditions, particularly once an executive and his or her team has become familiar with the structure and, most importantly, the associated thought process.

Review Appetite for Change

Once again, the organization's appetite for change should be confirmed. Most organizations can manage a maximum of five Issues simultaneously, which normally translates into three to five Strategies for each Issue and perhaps three to five Tactics per Strategy. Again, the numbers: a typical TAP features up to 25 Strategies and 125 Tactics. This activity will require staff time and dollars, much of which is not currently allocated in the budget. Budget and time constraints suggest the facilitator should make every attempt to drive the number of Strategies and Tactics to the essential few—those high-impact items required to resolve an Issue.

Stop-Doing List

The Stop-Doing List is precisely what it says: What activities can/should the organization stop doing? This may sound foolish, but it is an extremely informative exercise. By identifying things the organization can literally stop doing, the CPT will be able to identify time that is currently spent on less strategic activities, and shift it toward implementing the Plan.

Not only does this serve to focus the organization's attention and energy, it also provides an often much-needed check on the reasonableness of activities that may have lost their purpose but continue to be done because of inertia. Giving thought to this is time well spent and often a breath of fresh air for the entire staff. During this phase, one organization decided to stop collecting used clothing and equipment from its crews. This alleviated a staff action and follow-up requirement and allowed the crews to keep still useful (but not to job standards) items of clothing from time to time. Another more significant shift in thinking came when the discussion revealed the possibility to stop doing one-off project design and consider combining small projects into a more programmatic approach, thus allowing for more efficient use of consultants.

Core Work Functions

Core work functions represent the major duties and responsibilities of the organization. As an example, "maintain fleet vehicles" is a core work function, while "change vehicle sparkplugs" is not. Work functions can be internal or external in scope. For example, human resources activities are generally considered internal, whereas sales and customer relations are external. This exercise is best performed using breakout groups that are populated with CPT members having similar responsibilities. Typically, administrative, engineering, and operations are some of the more common work divisions.

Using self-adhesive notes, breakout groups should develop a list of work functions, one function per note. Each function should be stated concisely (less than four words) and should begin with an action verb. All notes should then be arranged on a wall according to work divisions. The CPT should eliminate duplicates and consider new functions that may result from the planning process. It is important to add the responsibility for leading and implementing the Strategic Leadership Plan as a core work function.

Furthermore, as part of the exercise of defining core work functions, the CPT should identify core competencies, which are those work functions that the organization cannot or should not outsource to consultants or vendors. Expertise is developed in-house. This exercise will test the CPT's bias and novophobia! Simply because there is a structural engineer on the payroll doesn't necessarily mean that designing infrastructure facilities is core to the overall operation. Nor does it mean that the structural engineer will be terminated if the function is not listed as a core work function. This phase of the process requires openness and critical thinking without defensiveness and the GM/CEO can play a key role in setting the stage for having this conversation.

Gap Analysis of Current Organization Chart

Following development of a list of draft core work functions and core competencies, the CPT should complete a gap analysis of the current organization chart. The objective of this analysis is to identify where current core work functions and competencies reside from an organizational perspective. If the CPT has followed the process, it should have identified new or revised core work functions and competencies. These new or revised items should next be evaluated in light of how or whether they fit within the current organizational structure. For example, one CPT identified "knowledge management" and "succession planning and staff transition" as future work functions. They decided that parts of these work functions fit within their current human resources group but that other parts might best align within various technical groups. The results of this gap analysis will be used for further work during CPT Workshop #6.

Workshop #6: Identifying the Champions

"Someone else is going to have to do this. I sure don't have the time."
Workshop Objective: Identify staff resources for plan implementation.

Prior to CPT Workshop #6, a few items need to be accomplished off-line. First of all, the meeting facilitator should discuss with the GM/CEO the attributes and role and responsibilities of Issue Sponsors. The facilitator may need to help identify a Sponsor for each Issue and perhaps talk with them individually prior to the meeting. Relative to this assignment, Sponsors will report to the person selected to manage the Strategic Leadership Plan and ongoing process, typically a member of the senior management.

Secondly, the facilitator should create Tactical Action Plan templates for the next CPT workshop. Thirdly, the GM/CEO and facilitator should discuss boundary conditions for adjusting the organization. Conditions may include collective bargaining, political and board considerations. Finally, the GM/CEO must identify the individual to manage the overall process going forward. Often the Change Agent, if not the CEO, is a leading candidate although considerations related to position, influence and workload are important.

The next employee meeting is important, as staff will be briefed on a number of ideas that may affect them personally, either directly or indirectly. It is rare that someone does not ask, "How many positions will be eliminated?" or "Is my job in jeopardy?" This is an entirely normal reaction to change and should be anticipated with a preplanned response. With the concurrence of the GM/CEO, the facilitator of the employee meeting should mention at the beginning that, when the plan is ultimately adopted, no positions will be eliminated. This action will go a long way toward removing the elephant from the room and enabling staff to engage in the process more openly.

WORKSHOP #6 AGENDA:

1. Review agenda
2. Review meeting notes from CPT Workshop #5
3. Modify/endorse core work functions and core competencies
4. Appoint Issue Sponsors, Strategy Champions, and SLP/TAP manager
5. Draft Strategies/Tactics for all Issues, including budgets, schedules, and deliverables
6. Prepare 2 or 3 alternative organizational models

Draft Tactics

The Issue Sponsors should facilitate individual breakout groups to draft Tactics for all Issues, with the balance of the CPT freely rotating among the groups during a one- to two-hour period. The number of Tactics permitted under each Strategy should be limited to no more than five. (Remember the numbers: if your organization tackles five Issues, staff will implement roughly 125 Tactics over a 12- to 18-month period.)

As with other plan elements, there is a sentence structure that is most effective when drafting Tactics. In this case a simple verb statement suffices, so an action word should begin each tactic. It is important to make sure that Tactics are more than a collection of softballs—items that are either a part of business as usual or that are already underway.

Subject matter experts can be invited to participate during the brainstorming portion of this meeting, to help generate outside-the-box ideas and provide technical advice. Issue Sponsors and Strategy Champions are responsible for filling in the template provided by the facilitator and for polishing/confirming the data off-line prior to the next CPT workshop. Although this information is rough and in draft form, the facilitator and GM/CEO should evaluate the collective budget and time impacts of the Tactics. This is where the rubber meets the road regarding the organization's appetite for change. Referring back to the Stop-Doing List will provide some thoughts on how to mitigate these impacts and concerns.

Draft Organizational Models

Core work functions and an organization chart gap analysis were generated during CPT Workshop #5. The CPT must now develop organizational models that account for this information. There are three basic choices: (1) draft models are created by the facilitator off-line, likely with input of the GM/CEO; (2) draft models are generated from scratch during CPT Workshop #6; or (3) draft models are developed during a senior management meeting. The approach chosen will be based upon the skills, dynamics, personal biases, and change appetite of the CPT. Since this discussion can be contentious and threatening to some members of the CPT, the facilitator must proceed with caution.

Three basic model options include the traditional "Do Nothing" version, a version with minor adjustments to the current organizational chart, and a third version with comprehensive changes to the organization. For example, a minor change may involve the addition of a Strategic Leadership Plan manager to a senior role in an existing organization chart. A broader, more comprehensive change could be proposed, although further organizational analysis may be required.

For each model, distribute the core work functions, as identified during CPT Workshop #6, to the appropriate positions. The current organization chart should be evaluated for span of control. The overall exercise should not focus on people, but on positions. Once positions are established and compared with the requirements of the SLP, they can be populated with people.

Changing organizational charts is routine for some organizations and rarely done by others. Organizations in the latter group should begin a tradition of making regular changes, albeit small, so that staff will consider the action culturally acceptable and routine. If small changes are acceptable now, the organization might take a more incremental approach to redesign the organization over time. The bottom line, however, is that if economic, social and political changes continue to mount on a regional, national and global level, organizations must change accordingly.

As the CPT considers draft organizational structures, keep in mind that there are two groups of stakeholders that will be viewing the organization chart; those internal to the organization and those who are external. Which group is more important? The answer to this question may impact the final result. For example, the graphic below shows two significantly different organizational structures for the same organization. One shows how the organization might be organized looking at people's jobs from an internal perspective. It aligns with work "disciplines" such as engineering, operations, etc. While this structure may be informative to those working within the organization, it may not be quite so evident to a customer who has a problem. In contrast, the second structure is aligned by "business units" or groupings of services that are provided by the organization. This type of structure is often more informative to customers and external stakeholders.

Work Discipline Organizational Model

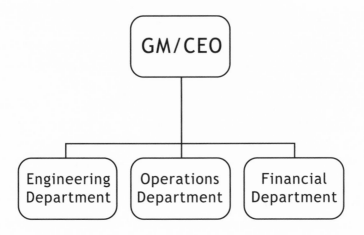

Business Line Organizational Model

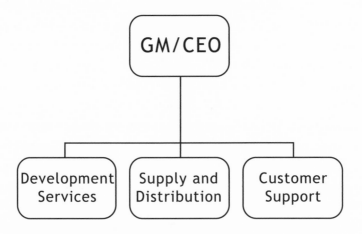

Workshop #7: Making Room for New Activities
"Maybe things *are* going to change."
Workshop Objective: Identify organizational changes
needed for implementation.

WORKSHOP #7 AGENDA:

1. Review agenda
2. Review meeting notes from CPT Workshop #6
3. Modify/endorse one organizational model
4. Review/modify draft Tactics
5. Update Stop-Doing List
6. Establish Early Wins List
7. Prepare for SMT, board, and all-hands meetings

Early Wins

Invariably, most organizations have undergone some sort of strategic planning process sometime in the past. The process most likely left a bad taste in the mouths of many, primarily because nothing changed. In fact, leadership may have since eliminated the phrase "strategic planning" from their vocabulary! The process used may have been either too theoretical, too cumbersome, or was labeled by staff as the flavor of the month or senior management's plan. Most likely, change did not occur because a cross section of employees did not have an opportunity to participate in the process.

Furthermore, the plan that was prepared may have adequately identified Issues and produced a lengthy list of objectives, but it came up short on producing a comprehensive action plan to implement the required change.

The attitude that nothing will change must quickly be reversed, even during the early stages of plan development. This can be accomplished using the concept of early wins. The CPT should develop this list, which identifies actions that can be completed within 90 days or less. Ideas can be drawn from the list of Tactics and from the Stop-Doing List. Ideally, the CPT can identify a few items to recommend to the SMT, board, and staff for immediate implementation. The impacts of these actions may be small, but if they are properly communicated, staff will quickly recognize that change is occurring. For example, one organization identified development of a consistent cell phone policy as an early win.

Early wins include both easy-to-accomplish and more challenging items. The purpose is twofold. First, the process itself identifies items that are both urgent and quite doable; the team agrees there is no time to waste. Secondly, there are items that are perhaps not urgent, but that are visibly positive within the organization, such as the cell phone policy cited above. In either case, the point is to show early success and build understanding that there really is going to be change. Examples of early wins include:

- Develop and issue department cell phone policy.
- Retain consultant to develop space plan for more efficient office configuration.
- Include SLP/TAP status report as a regular board of directors agenda item.

Employee Meeting—Reiterate Endorsement

Following CPT Workshop #6, another employee meeting should be held. The agenda basically remains the same as in previous sessions. Staff should be briefed on the current version of elements developed to date including the Vision, Issues, Goals, Strategies, Tactics, Values, core work functions, core competencies, organizational models, Stop-Doing List, and Early Wins List. Emphasis should be placed on capturing staff input on the draft Tactics. The length of this meeting will necessarily be longer than the first. At the end of the meeting, the facilitator should ask those attending for an endorsement vote. Remember, planning obeys the law of diminishing returns and strives for 80 percent accuracy, with the associated requirement that plans are updated on an annual basis or sooner as conditions dictate. Endorsement means that those attending find merit with the plan and its content. Furthermore, they agree to support, or at least to not oppose, the process and, where possible, help with implementation.

Workshop #8: Taking Care of the Details

"This is really coming together."
Workshop Objective: Finalize the detailed work plan.

WORKSHOP #8 AGENDA:

1. Review agenda
2. Review meeting notes from CPT Workshop #7
3. Discuss input received from board, SMT, and staff
4. Modify/edit Issues, Goals, Strategies, Vision and Values
5. Modify/edit Tactics
6. Confirm appetite for change
7. Develop draft job descriptions for key positions
8. Draft Performance Metrics
9. Develop draft process diagrams
10. Discuss format of SLP and TAP and make writing assignments

Key Position Job Descriptions

Most organizations have job descriptions for key positions. The CPT needs to review these to ensure they account for the core work functions identified earlier in the process, in that these functions translate into responsibilities. Job descriptions should contain approximately six primary and six secondary responsibilities, and include individual Performance Metrics that are in alignment with the organization's Performance Metrics. In other words, the core work functions (responsibilities) and Performance Metrics found in the Strategic Leadership Plan should cascade down into individual job descriptions.

Job descriptions, which should define specific roles, responsibilities and metrics, are normally written for management and most staff. Should similar documents be written for members of the board? We say yes. This book contains a separate chapter on board governance; organizations perform significantly better if board members, management and staff are full participants in implementing the plan.

Performance Metrics

Performance Metrics are interesting to develop, but normally difficult to install in an organization not familiar with measuring performance or enforcing accountability—this is another root cause of the complaint that nothing ever changes. If Performance Metrics are well conceived, the entire organization, from the boardroom to the field, can instantly determine whether Strategies are having a positive impact on operations. Performance Metrics are normally presented in graphic form and measure performance results over time.

The CPT should identify one Performance Metric for each Issue. Additional Performance Metrics can be developed in subsequent years. This focused approach contrasts yet again with many others that produce a small telephone book of metrics, and require an army to maintain them on a monthly or quarterly basis. A rule to remember: The more complex a metric, the more likely accuracy and credibility will suffer. Strive for simplicity and keep the metric at a strategic level during this important exercise. The key question is, "What impact will all Strategies identified for an Issue have on the organization?"

The focus on simplicity cannot be overemphasized when establishing Performance Metrics. Some items can even be measured by a simple pass/fail test. For example, an activity either got completed by a certain date or it didn't. Many items can be numerically measured in terms of a percentage decrease in cost, percentage increase in customer satisfaction, or percentage of time saved. These can easily be communicated to senior management and the board using a graphic format, as illustrated in the example.

Example Performance Metric

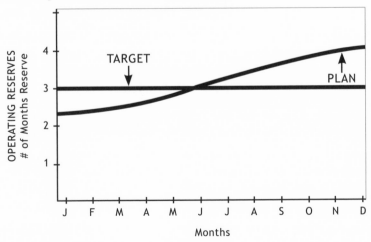

Perhaps the most difficult items to measure are those that produce intangible results. For example, how could an organization wishing to improve customer service or employee morale measure results over time? One method is to use surveys that ask respondents to rate various attributes on a scale of 1 to 5. The first time the survey is completed would establish a baseline score for each attribute. The same survey could be issued 6, 12 or 24 months later. If progress had been made, each of the attributes would have a better aggregate score than the original baseline.

Process Diagrams

The loss of institutional knowledge is becoming a major issue for most organizations, especially as the baby boom generation moves into retirement. Senior managers around the country must contend with the loss of vital information once key resources walk out the door, due to retirement or other employment opportunities. One way to counter this loss is to develop comprehensive process diagrams for all critical core work functions.

A few organizations have developed detailed Standard Operating Procedures, which are typically long on text and contain only rudimentary process diagrams, if any. Unfortunately, these documents are typically targeted for use by the human resources department and are rarely updated or used in training sessions. Still other organizations have turned to ISO certification, a rigorous and time-consuming process that is generally required for doing work outside the United States, to ensure that work functions are properly documented. *The Art of Strategic Leadership* promotes a solution that takes a middle ground, somewhere between text-heavy SOPs and ISO certification.

For this part of the workshop, each breakout group is assigned a core work function. They should be given an example of a well constructed process diagram and instructed to follow suit. With little direction, the resulting diagrams are usually thorough and logically presented. These process diagrams should be featured in regular training sessions and updated frequently.

Example Process Diagram

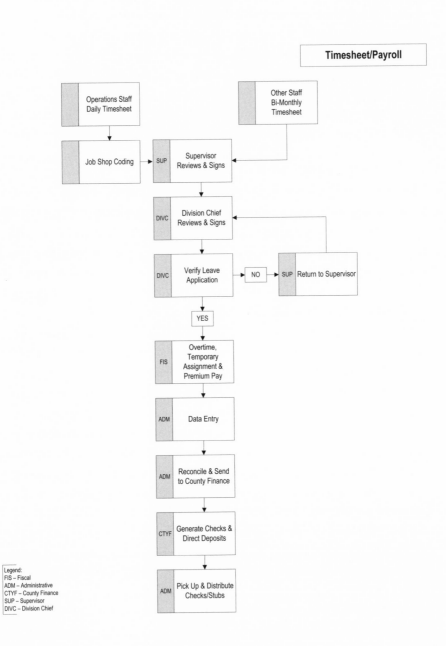

Timesheet/Payroll

Operations Staff Daily Timesheet

Other Staff Bi-Monthly Timesheet

Job Shop Coding

SUP — Supervisor Reviews & Signs

DIVC — Division Chief Reviews & Signs

DIVC — Verify Leave Application → NO → SUP — Return to Supervisor

YES

FIS — Overtime, Temporary Assignment & Premium Pay

ADM — Data Entry

ADM — Reconcile & Send to County Finance

CTYF — Generate Checks & Direct Deposits

ADM — Pick Up & Distribute Checks/Stubs

Legend:
FIS – Fiscal
ADM – Administrative
CTYF – County Finance
SUP – Supervisor
DIVC – Division Chief

Workshop #9: Finalizing the TAP

"Now I really know things are going to change around here."
Workshop Objective: Finalize the plan and prepare for its implementation.

WORKSHOP #9 AGENDA:
1. Review agenda
2. Review meeting notes from CPT Workshop #8
3. Review/endorse job descriptions for key positions
4. Review/endorse Performance Metrics
5. Review/modify process diagrams
6. Review draft SLP and TAP
7. Develop consolidated schedule for completing all Tactics contained in TAP
8. Develop schedule for updating SLP/TAP
9. Develop communication plan
10. Prepare for SMT and board meetings

Elements of a Communication Plan

When it comes to communication, more is almost always better. In fact, it is safe to say that organizations are always more effective if there is a good degree of healthy communication. At no time is this truer than when initiating organizational change. In fact, there will be communication—and a good deal of it—regarding the efforts underway. The only question is whether the organization chooses to take charge of the nature and accuracy of the communication or leave it to the rumor mill. Obviously the best approach is for the leaders to get their message out. This serves to engage stakeholders, decrease confusion, limit anxiety and build enthusiasm.

The Art of Strategic Leadership intends for CPT members to take on a lead communication role. That is, in their role on the CPT, these staff members have also agreed to serve as a communication conduit back to the organization, sharing progress, soliciting feedback and building buy-in. After each CPT session, the team is assigned this task. However, in some organizations, the CPT does not serve effectively in this role for a variety of reasons, including:

- CPT members are uncomfortable with a role in communication.
- Such communication is not the cultural norm for the organization.
- CPT members lack confidence.

Whatever the reasons, if the recommended communication between the CPT and the broader staff is not happening or is not having the desired effect, supplemental communication is essential. It is the communication to the broader staff that builds 100 percent endorsement of the plan going forward, so circumventing this step creates a fatal flaw to the entire process. In fact, communication is so critical that even with the CPT fulfilling its role, an organization may want to consider using other methods as well. Other commonly used communication methods include employee newsletters and employee meetings or focus groups. The newsletter is most effective if it is published after each CPT workshop, or at least monthly. The rumor mill flourishes in voids, so it is best to keep the information flowing on a regular basis. This can be a newsletter published specifically for this purpose, or a feature in an existing monthly in-house newsletter. In either case, the items to be covered include:

- Purpose of the change process
- Process summary to date
- Basic definitions
- Plan elements as drafted
- Names of the CPT members
- Solicitation of comments and feedback

Another important communication effort involves regular all-hands meetings where employees can engage in dialog about the process and the plan itself. Although CPT members or the GM/CEO can lead these sessions, some organizations prefer outside facilitation. In either case, these sessions should be held after CPT Workshops #2, #5 and #8. The purpose of these meetings is to present progress to date, engage in dialog and capture input. This feedback is then taken back to the next CPT workshop as a basis for refining the plan itself. Both soliciting and acting on the feedback are essential elements of building trust across the broader organization. This level of trust is essential for endorsement of the plan and for the staff support necessary for successful implementation. Whoever is asked to facilitate these employee sessions, it is important to hold a neutral posture—that is, no defensiveness allowed. These sessions are not the place to solve problems or defend positions, but to communicate about the process, clarify if possible and capture input to take back to the planning process. The basic agenda for an all-hands meeting is:

- Introduction and opening remarks
- Review purpose of session
- Establish session ground rules (if necessary)
- Review elements of plan developed to date, noting areas of focus for this session
- Provide a detailed review of elements
- Capture employee input on flip charts
- Seek endorsement
- Outline next steps and methodology for ongoing employee input

One more simple way to communicate is to develop an employee comment box specific to this effort. The form for comments should include not only a comment but also a suggested solution as a way to engage all employees in not only outlining problems, but thinking of solutions for moving forward.

These communication activities should keep employees, the board, stakeholders and customers informed on efforts to implement the SLP/TAP. In particular, these weekly or monthly publications will reverse the collective reaction of staff to previous processes: "Nothing changed." Emphasis should be placed on early wins.

Workshop #10: Final Cleanup

"We've come a long way and change is going to happen."
Workshop Objective: Endorse the plan and celebrate success.

WORKSHOP #10 AGENDA:

1. Review agenda
2. Review meeting notes from CPT Workshop #9
3. Discuss input received from SMT and board
4. Review/modify/endorse SLP and TAP
5. Endorse communication plan
6. Conduct post-mortem, review/adjust planning process
7. Celebrate success!
8. Turn directly to Implementation

Implementation Starts Now

Celebrate success? Not quite so fast! Yes, the team has achieved a real milestone. However, we all know that real success only happens with effective implementation. It is vital to see the planning and implementation phases of the process as a linked set—it is not possible to successfully turn the plan into a solution without turning directly to focused implementation. In fact, not only is it important to start implementation, but it is important to start it quickly in order to build on the momentum and get visible in relation to the early wins identified previously. Now, the real work finally starts!

4

Implementation
The Critical
Element

Now we come to the step that separates the organizational success stories from the others: Implementation. The phase of the process where the richness of the work completed so far is revealed. This is the most rewarding aspect of the process because here we begin to witness real organizational change. And this is another important point in the journey where *The Art of Strategic Leadership* departs from the norm and produces superior results.

The simple truth is the essential element lacking in most planning processes is attention and intention during the implementation phase. Although one can often identify subtle positive changes that may have resulted from the group dynamics during the planning process, the targeted results called for in the Strategic Leadership Plan (SLP) simply will not happen without clear, concentrated and accountable effort.

Creating Clear, Concentrated and Accountable Effort

The Art of Strategic Leadership drives from a generalized and conceptual look at organizational direction—Vision, Mission, and Values—through increasing focus on Issues, Goals, Strategies and Performance Metrics that ultimately result in actionable Tactical Action Plans (TAPs). *The Art of Strategic Leadership* recommends the implementation phase should take the TAP one step further into creation and implementation of highly specific Task Plans.

Hallmarks of successful Task Plans include:

- Clarity: Implementation is not left to individual interpretation or "fudge factor" accomplishment. The tasks, assignments and deadlines are clearly detailed.
- Focus: Like the planning process itself, the implementation phase is focused in time and effort to create the energy necessary for success and to create measurable change that is directly aligned with the planning direction.
- Accountability: With crystal clear assignments stating who is responsible for what to happen and by when, organizations can close the often elusive accountability loop.

Developing Actionable Task Plans

Not surprisingly, the cornerstones to developing effective Task Plans are the people who have been assigned during the previous planning process. Although Task Plan development can be accomplished in a variety of ways, the most efficient method to get these done is to rely on the plan process facilitator and Issue/Strategy leadership teams. As during the planning process itself, the facilitator takes on the role of catalyzing action so that forward movement continues. Many times, organizations have staff assigned that is entirely capable and motivated to develop the Task Plans and move toward implementation.

However, the assigned staff members usually already have full-time jobs.

In order to sustain the focus necessary to write the Task Plans and start actual plan implementation, the process facilitator is often in the best position to act as the support system for the organization. The facilitator can be internal or external to the organization, although experience has shown that external leads are often most effective due to process experience and the ability to focus their efforts. In either case, the facilitator should take on the following tasks:

- Schedule meetings with Issues Sponsors and Strategy Champions.
- Brainstorm and discuss detailed ideas regarding implementation by tactical area.
- Document the Task Plans adding insight and sequencing as the Task Plan writing process moves forward.
- Detail the data needs and availability for tracking according to the Performance Metrics as called for in the SLP.
- Develop a schedule that balances action with organizational tolerance.
- Schedule and conduct review meetings with Strategy/Tactic teams.
- Finalize the Task Plans for immediate implementation.

Commitment and Follow-Through

Throughout *The Art of Strategic Leadership*, a commitment is being made to the broader organization. The work that is done is highly visible and inclusive by design, so there is an expectation that is developed across the organization. Staff will hold the CPT and board to their promises and expect that the commitments made will be kept.

In fact, *not* acting as indicated in the SLP will surely undermine the credibility of the CPT and senior leadership, thus negatively impacting morale. This further underscores the importance of an implementation process that is balanced to the capabilities and capacity of the organization. Note that the capabilities and capacity of the organization include both internal resources and additional resources hired through possible new staff or consulting engagements. It is useful to think broadly about how the SLP can be accomplished and what resources can be mobilized toward addressing the Issues so that success is ensured.

The degree of internal staffing and external support varies among organizations. While some agencies have sufficient staff with broad business skills to handle many aspects of SLP implementation, others are quite lean and more narrowly focused on the technical aspects of running a utility enterprise. Therefore, the critical right resource mix for SLP implementation must be tailored according to organizational needs and capabilities.

In some cases, the governing board may have provided virtually full-time consultant support during SLP implementation knowing that staff was too thin to accomplish the required tasks. At the other end of the spectrum, organizations may choose to implement entirely on their own with only periodic facilitator check-ins to monitor performance to plan and create a soft accountability loop. Only the most focused and business-oriented organizations have been capable of implementing without ongoing facilitator support. Since the stakes are high in this regard, this option should be taken only with certainty that the SLP can be implemented using a strong internal lead with sufficient time to commit and with a high degree of internal authority.

Engaging the Entire Organization

The entire organization can and should have the opportunity to be involved in SLP implementation. There is plenty of work to be done, and tapping the resources of the entire organization is a powerful tool. Depending on staff size, this involvement can be highly individualized or accomplished through group meetings. Either through one-on-one interviews or a larger meeting format, the dialog should turn from:

"What are our organizational issues and how might we address them?"

to:

"How can we be most successful implementing the plan and what can you personally contribute?"

The degree to which the broader organization is engaged is part of the "art" in *The Art of Strategic Leadership*. The art is found in understanding the needs of the organization and what would be most effective. While one fairly small organization that struggles with accountability needed extensive individual involvement and buy-in, another larger more complex utility needed only continued organization-wide briefing updates and open dialog sessions. At either end of the spectrum, success is found in continuous focus and a degree of engagement that touches all staff.

An example from one end of the spectrum: For one organization that struggles with apathy and lacks accountability, the manager and external planning process facilitators individually distributed plan documents and got initials from individuals to acknowledge their receipt of the documents. This was followed by individual interviews conducted by the facilitator to ask the question framed above.

Because of particularly low morale in this organization, staff often wanted to continue to inventory the problems within the organization during these one-on-one interviews. They had failed to recognize that once the efforts turned to SLP implementation, this was no longer the point. Although the first phases of the planning process, particularly Issues identification, builds from understanding what's wrong, the implementation phase is entirely forward looking. As such, these dialogs were re-focused to what could be done next. Although staff was in the habit of complaining, the implementation interviews were focused on the future and each individual's role for making a contribution. This sometimes required firmly guided dialog, and represented an opportunity to reinforce the message that the organization was only interested in moving forward. Similar messaging applies whether in an individual interview format or larger group meetings.

Whatever the process used, from individual interviews to larger group meetings, the point is to get each person to commit to some kind of support of the SLP implementation. This commitment can range from simply stating an area of interest to agreeing to serve on a task implementation team. In order to reinforce this support and commitment, each person is therefore asked to attach their name to one of the Issue areas identified in the SLP. You can create a simple summary list or diagram of the Issues to provide a mechanism for presenting the highlights of the plan and gathering staff interest. This can be used in individual interviews or as a poster-sized sign-up for larger group meetings to create inclusiveness and build interest.

Designing Balance into Implementation

Utility organizations are filled with highly productive, accomplished and capable individuals. As such, there is a tendency during Task Plan development sessions to want to do it all. There is a key role here for the facilitator to build on that enthusiasm while insisting on a dose of organizational reality. The balance between these two varies among organizations. While some organizations will need a push to do more, others will need the reins pulled in to be sure they can accomplish what they commit to.

Identifying Highest Leverage Points

After the initial planning process is completed and implementation has begun, it is time to validate the priorities established in the SLP. Often the Strategies assigned as critical are in fact those highest leverage points, but sometimes there are too many of them to accomplish in the initial effort. If this is the case, it does not mean that the items are not critical, but may mean that there are some that can be deemed as the highest leverage points and should therefore be addressed first. Hallmarks of the highest leverage points are:

- Strong themes that emerge from individual interviews or group briefings
- Areas that the senior leadership and process facilitator agree are the first of the many critical items identified
- Points that, when addressed, will create the most visible and highest-impact improvement to the organization

The point is to address those specific tactical items that will create change and demonstrate to the entire organization that things indeed shall change as a result of this SLP. Organizational leadership must demonstrate that it is not novophobic and has the fortitude to lead the charge. There is a window of opportunity here for modeling behavior that can permeate the entire organization in this time of change and will having lasting positive impact.

It is important that selected critical, high leverage actions get underway within the first 60 days of SLP implementation. This demonstrates senior leadership's intent to implement the plan while showing the entire organization that it has the will to make the tough decisions to impact change. These high leverage items usually are not secrets within an organization, particularly after the broad involvement that has been included in developing the SLP itself.

In some cases, organizations conduct wholesale organizational redesign as a result of this process and start those more critical items immediately. For example, one planning process revealed a gap in customer service between the desired state and actual service delivery. One of the highest leverage points identified and addressed as a result was a customer service audit and implementation of a redesign that included reassignment of the department manager and hiring of a more effective leader for that critical role. In another instance, there was severe abuse of hours and time reporting by the field operations division, so the highest leverage point identified was a timesheet audit to document the Issue, immediate implementation of supervisory training. The organization also took steps to set the expectation that disciplinary procedures related to on-time attendance and honest time reporting would be enforced across the organization. Another company identified that it did not have the right sales and marketing support team to achieve the growth targets it had outlined, so adjustments were made including both reassignment and hiring of key staff in that area.

In the examples above, note that significant personnel changes resulted based on the fact that the correct leadership was lacking. Although this is not *always* the case with the highest leverage point Tactics, it is *often* the case. Make no mistake—staff is watching. This approach serves to underscore the importance that senior leadership is placing on the SLP with clearly demonstrable change. By the way, these changes are often ones that many others in the organization have already realized the need for. Taking such action, if required, builds leadership's reputation and focuses organizational attention. Again, this is not always the case and should not be forced if not required. However, if such changes are required, shying away from decisive action will undermine the plan and senior leadership itself.

In the case of one company, the executive team identified a need and implemented a far-reaching corporate branding effort. As is typical, such a change was met with a portion of staff who were willing to get on board, a portion who were waiting for proof and a portion who were resistant. And, as always, leadership had a choice to make—either play to the critics and pull back on the direction or forge ahead with confidence and make it clear that this was the direction the company was heading in. Because the leadership decisively stayed the course, the majority of the staff became supportive and the resistance was minimized. Working with a decisive direction and leveraging the staff who are ready for change can make all the difference.

Planning makes a visible commitment to the organization and sets an expectation for constructive change. Implementation is where the rubber meets the road. Failing here most certainly undermines leadership and reinforces apathy.

Looping Back on Early Wins

In addition to the high leverage action items that will be underway within the first 60 days of SLP implementation, there are other items that demonstrate intent and create success but are perhaps less involved and extensive.

During the planning process, some early wins were likely identified and acted upon. The first 60 days of plan implementation creates another opportunity to address the next layer of urgent actions with a particular focus on those that can move change forward with concise actions. So, in the initial development of Task Plans, such items should also be identified.

An example of an early win, described previously in Chapter 3, involved developing a cell phone policy where none had existed previously. The task was fairly straightforward and involved minimal time commitment for a small task team to develop a recommendation for senior management's review and approval. For that organization a minimal investment in time paid a major dividend by demonstrating a clear commitment to SLP implementation.

The following excerpt from a Strategic Leadership Plan illustrates the highly specific nature of the Task Plans. Such detail is developed for each and every Strategy/Tactic set defined in the Plan and illustrates the nature of the Task Plan detail discussed above.

Sample Tactical Action Plan

Issue 1 / Strategy 4 / Tactic 1

Sponsor: Albert Johnson   **Champion:** Kathy Green   **Priority:** Strategy – Medium
Tactic – Medium

Issue	A skilled and knowledgeable workforce must be attracted, developed and retained

Strategy	An aggressive recruitment program attracts the most qualified workforce

Tactic	Participate in external job fairs

Tasks	1. Form a committee 2. Identify job fairs/conferences relevant to our industry 3. Develop a kiosk/booth and promotional material 4. Develop rotation of department representatives to staff booth 5. Communicate recommendations 6. Implement 7. Evaluate program
Key Decision Points	
Dependencies	Staff availability
Resources	Department heads/managers and other team members

Schedule	Milestones
Jan '09	Form a committee (36 hours)
Feb '09 – Mar '09	Identify job fairs/conferences relevant to our industry (96 hours)
Apr '09 – Aug '09	Develop a kiosk/booth and promotional material and develop rotation of department representatives to staff booth – maybe some recruitment requirement (300 hours)
Sep '09	Communicate recommendations (12 hours)
Jan '10	Implement (48 hours)
May '10 & Nov '10	Evaluate program (48 hours)

Budget	Hours	Labor	Direct Materials	Other	Total	Comments
FY 08/09	444	$12,432			$12,432	
FY 09/10	48	$1,344			$1,344	

Note the following features of well-crafted Task Plans:
- Actions are highly specific and assigned.
- Teams are clearly defined and cross-functional within the organization.
- Deadlines are clear.
- Additional budget requirements are specified.
- Schedules are realistic.

Continuing the Focus

Although not always the case, leaders tend to be highly motivated and driven personalities with a tendency to quickly move on to the next urgent item. Staying focused on SLP implementation without being distracted is critical and can run contrary to organizational habits. In fact, many organizations are crisis-driven, which creates a disconnect relative to the ability to plan in the first place, let alone stay the course on SLP implementation.

As such, after the initial 60-day implementation push where a few visible critical items are addressed and a couple of early wins are added to the mix, it is important to settle into a consistent routine. This routine means that accountability to SLP implementation becomes part of business as usual. Thinking about and acting on the plan is woven into the fabric of the organization. This is seen as a basic element of the Plan and is incorporated in the expected dialog at leadership team meetings, staff briefings, internal communications and other venues that indicate integration into the very culture of the organization.

Addressing Communication...Again

Where would a chapter on creating the change necessary for strategic leadership be without yet another word on communication? *The Art of Strategic Leadership* is founded on a rigorous communication process because it is so critical to building the broad understanding and buy-in necessary for full endorsement.

But this is only the beginning. The vast majority of Strategic Leadership Plans that have been written feature an Issue related to communication. Experience has shown time and again that communication is always lacking, always imperfect and always in need of improvement. So, it is likely that the plan itself includes specific Issues, Strategies and Tactics related to communication in some way or another. For example, in one SLP communication was nested in an Issue stated as, "Employee morale must be improved." It is difficult to improve morale without improving communication.

The implementation phase is merely a continuation of the planning process. Although the Change Agent, Issues Sponsors and key organizational leadership may continue to understand the connection between the SLP and the activities related to implementation, the broader organization simply will not "get it" unless those connections are reinforced through effective communication.

To illustrate, during the individual interviews related to initial SLP implementation, one employee commented that nothing had happened yet, even though we had talked about early wins during the planning phase. This organization struggled with low morale and the plan called for enhanced communication with employees. During the planning itself, several initiatives were started including a suggestion box and monthly newsletter. The day prior to this interview, the first of regular monthly employee meetings was held. However, this employee could not see this. The dots were not being connected.

It is the job of leadership and part of SLP implementation to connect those dots, to tell employees precisely what is happening as a result of the plan. Expecting each individual employee to recall the details of the plan, to see the connection of tactical implementation back to the SLP, and then to even recall that connection over time is simply unrealistic. Therefore, SLP implementation must include clear communication regarding progress to plan on a regular basis. Again, as woven into the fabric of the organization, this becomes part of all conversations with employees including:

- Newsletters
- Staff meetings (group and department level)
- Project planning
- Performance reviews
- Executive briefings
- Other communication vehicles specific to an organization

Making the Grade

As part of an annual summary evaluation of the organization's progress on its SLP, it is useful to do a self-evaluation based on the familiar A through F grading system. Through dialog with the Issue Sponsors, implementation team and leadership team, a grade on performance to date should be developed. This forces another accountability loop in the subsequent use of that grade in a summary back to the entire organization regarding how things are progressing. An honest assessment is important here and the dialog in assigning the grade is as important as the grade itself. A report card with all A's is not likely, so the team must hold itself accountable during this discussion, again a place where an outside perspective can be helpful.

5

Governance
Getting the Board on Board

Within most public agencies that provide infrastructure-related services, the board of directors, or its governing equivalent, is ultimately answerable for the performance and activities of the entire organization. This section has been written with a focus on public agencies, but most principles can be adapted by private-sector companies as well.

Boards play a critical role in providing the strategic leadership necessary to assure that the change process is complete and sustainable. If the role of the board is that critical, the board itself may need to make some changes in its behavior to increase the likelihood that the organization will achieve success.

All too often, boards micromanage the organizations they oversee. We have observed boards spending hours of their valuable time discussing the merits of proposed office equipment purchases, editing technical reports, or delving into design details of capital projects, details for which staff should be responsible. They do this for a variety of reasons. Some board members may have a particular area of technical expertise and feel their input or attention is adding value. Some may feel their attention to detail demonstrates their managerial prowess. Others may simply not understand what their role is as a board member. The example behaviors described are symptomatic of an operational board, that is, a board that gets directly involved in the day-to-day activities and decisions of the organization.

To be fair, boards sometimes must get involved in operational details, especially if the organization lacks a general manager or if circumstances threaten the financial or legal well being of the organization. However, in the majority of cases the boards of high-performance organizations have been able to make the transition from dealing with operational issues to establishing strategic goals for the organization and identifying policies necessary to achieve the Strategic Direction. Once they have achieved this, they have successfully made the transition from an operational board to a policy board.

Special Challenges to Energizing the Board for Change

Leading a board through a change process may present special challenges.

Scheduling times to meet with the board can present logistical challenges because of open meeting laws that regulate how and when public boards may assemble as a group. Special attention needs to be paid to restrictions on the venue and frequency of board meetings, public notification requirements, duration of available interaction time with the board, and how information may be presented to and received from board members. Therefore, the steps for leading a public board through a change process must consider these special requirements well in advance of scheduling meetings.

Board members may come from widely diverse backgrounds and they often have different understandings of their role as an individual member of the board. Surprisingly, individual board members sometimes do not fully understand the day-to-day business of the organization that they oversee. As a result, it is often necessary to guide them through a process to help them coalesce as a group and identify their common direction.

Because board members are typically appointed or elected, and may have term limits, the composition of the board can be transitory in nature. Therefore, it is critical that written board roles and policies be developed and adopted to identify how board members are to interact among themselves and how they are to communicate with and monitor the organization that they oversee. Often, this information does not exist.

It is common to encounter elected city or county council members who have been appointed to serve on the governing board of a public infrastructure utility or agency. This practice can result in a political environment that impacts how board members interact and make decisions, and may impede the board's ability to operate as an efficient unit.

Addressing the Board's Appetite for Change

Just as with senior management and staff, it is essential that the board come to grips with its appetite for change. Changes within the organization inevitably require changes in how the board behaves as a group, where and how it focuses its energy moving forward, and how it interacts with the rest of the organization. If the board has been actively participating in the change process described in this book it should already be energized and receptive to the concept of identifying how changes in its own behavior can be channeled for the betterment of the organization as a whole. However, like some members of the Core

Planning Team, board members may find themselves experiencing various levels of novophobia (fear of change) when confronted with the clear need for change.

One tool that has proven to be highly effective for implementing change within a board is to lead it through a process of developing board governance policies. Governance policies outline the span of authority and control of the board as well as that of the organization's management and staff. They provide the critical structure needed to help a board in its transition from an operational board to a policy board.

Boards that have chosen to take themselves through the process of developing governance policies have typically found the experience extremely valuable because they accomplish the following:

- They often find they are better able to coalesce as a group by defining and clarifying their role in the change process.
- They have found it easier to orient new members to their roles as individuals and the role of the board as a group.
- They have found they are able to reduce the amount of time they must spend at board meetings, and that the time they do spend is more productive.
- They demonstrate to management and staff that the board also recognizes and values the need to change.

Getting Started

As noted earlier, legal restrictions and other considerations may pose special challenges when working with public boards. Finding the time in a busy board's schedule to focus on developing governance policies is another logistical issue. In presenting options to a board for scheduling time needed to develop governance policies, there are two primary options. Some boards may prefer a brute-force approach wherein they schedule a two-day facilitated work session and they hammer their way through the steps needed to identify their appetite for change and develop governance policies accordingly. This approach requires board members to be constantly on their toes over the course of the two days and can be quite exhausting for all concerned. Using this approach, a significant amount of information must be digested and processed over a short period of time; this is an experience akin to drinking water from a fire hose.

A more preferable approach is to schedule a minimum two-hour work session during or after each of three consecutive regularly scheduled board meetings. While this approach results in a longer overall time frame, it offers several advantages:

- First, individual board members often find this approach easier to schedule and less disruptive to their lives outside of the boardroom.
- Second, it provides time for the board to assimilate and consider the information as it is developed, resulting in a better final work product. With this schedule, interim deliverables capture information developed during the previous session(s), and it provides board members with the time necessary to review the information.
- Third, it provides time for information to gel and for board members to ask themselves and perhaps others, "How is this going to impact the board as a group, what changes in behavior will be required of me personally, and do we really want to do this?"

Note that the work of developing policies is sensitive in nature. Items under discussion or in process can be damaging to organizational morale or community perception, often unnecessarily as they are taken out of context or only to be discussed as options then discarded. For these reasons, the best approach may be to discuss and develop some policies in executive, closed session.

Sample Work Session Agendas

The sections that follow provide sample agendas, including objectives and suggested deliverables, for separate work sessions spanning three consecutive board meetings. The agendas are designed to help a board determine its appetite for change and develop a set of draft board governance policies.

As noted above, unless there is a driving need for a quick turn-around on identifying draft governance policies, we recommend a three-session approach. However, the same information could easily be adapted for use in a back-to-back two-day work session.

Board Governance Work Session No. 1
Objectives: The objectives of this work session include establishing the board's objectives regarding governance policies, identifying existing policies and state or other regulatory authority that may impact future governance policies, and identifying the information needed to prepare a rough draft set of governance policies.

Activities:
- Identify how the board currently governs its activities, including its understanding of its roles and responsibilities as a board, as individual board members, the role of the GM/CEO, and how the board interacts with staff.
- Compare and contrast the key differences between an operational board and a policy board, and identify the advantages and disadvantages of each form of governance structure.
- Facilitate a gap analysis to help the board identify current conditions within the organization and desired future conditions.
- Identify on a preliminary basis the level of authority the board is comfortable delegating to its GM/CEO and the level of authority the board wishes to retain.
- Identify the primary components of the proposed policy governance model, including examples of governance policies adopted by other similar organizations. Identify governance issues that may be specific to this board. Explore the board's reactions to sample governance policies of others (their likes and dislikes, etc.).
- Suggest that the board request an opinion from its legal counsel as to any items in existing board policies or bylaws, state enabling statutes, or other legal issues that would preclude or

impact the board's ability to prepare and adopt governance policies for itself.

It is critical that the board members have an honest discussion among themselves about how they currently govern the organization. This discussion should include a comparison of the differences between an operational board and a policy board. When they first hear these terms, many boards get confused with one of their roles of making and adopting board policies and respond with "we are both." The following table presents a comparison of the characteristics of an operational board and a policy board that may be useful in these discussions.

Operational Board vs. Policy Board

Operational Board	Policy Board

• Engages in operational issues
• Brainstorms operational solutions
• Debates operational decisions
• Metrics unclear or non-existent
• GM/CEO and staff have lower levels of authority
• Reactive governance structure
	• Thinks strategically
	  - Future trends
	  - Upcoming threats
	  - Proactive strategies
	• Delegates authority to GM/CEO
	• Criteria and metrics well defined
	• Continuously educating itself
	• Board and GM/CEO understand:
	  - Roles and responsibilities
	  - Lines of authority
	  - Expectations
	• GM/CEO held accountable for results
	• Proactive governance structure

During the work session, discussion needs to stress that to provide strategic leadership and assure the organization's success in implementing the Strategic Leadership Plan/Tactical Action Plan (SLP/TAP), the board must shift from acting as an operational board to a policy board that provides strategic direction for the organization, instructs its GM/CEO to achieve certain performance goals, and then continuously monitors results.

The governance policy model used in this book has been adapted after *Reinventing Your Board*, by Dr. John Carver. The model focuses on the use of four quadrants to help define board governance activities. The governance quadrants are shown in the following figure.

Board Policy Governance Model

A brief description of the primary elements of each quadrant of the model follows:

- Board Governance Policies: This quadrant defines the board's instructions to itself in terms of how it will act as a board, including behavior of its individual members and committees. The board also defines its overall purpose in this section.
- Board–GM/CEO Policies: In this section the board describes how it will transfer authority to the GM/CEO and describes

how it will monitor performance. The power of the model lies in the way that accountability for achieving results along with the necessary authority is transferred from the board to the GM/CEO. The board's sole mechanism for communicating to the organization is through the GM/CEO, eliminating the micromanaging of staff that often occurs with operational boards.

- GM/CEO Limitation Policies: Here, the board instructs the GM/CEO as to what specific actions or activities are to be *avoided.* In other words, instead of providing an exhaustive list of things the GM/CEO must do, the board specifies what the GM/CEO cannot do. The implication is obvious: if an activity is not specifically prohibited then reasonable interpretation of the policy says it is permitted. This is an incredibly empowering policy for the GM/CEO, particularly when combined with Strategic Direction policies that define what the GM/CEO is to achieve.

- Board Strategic Direction: This set of policies requires the board to instruct the GM/CEO as to its future expectations for the organization and what the GM/CEO is to achieve. A clear distinction is that the board defines what results are to be achieved, but not how the GM/CEO is to achieve them.

Using information gathered during the first work session with the board, a set of draft governance policies should be prepared. They should be distributed to board members sufficiently in advance of the second work session so that members can review them and identify areas for questions or revisions.

Board Governance Work Session No. 2
Objectives: The objectives of the second work session include presenting, discussing and modifying, as necessary, rough draft board governance policies and development of draft information needed to support implementation and sustain the governance policies.

Activities:

- Review discussions from the previous work session. Legal counsel should report on any issues related to enabling legislation or other areas of legal concern regarding development of board governance policies.

- Review the rough draft board governance policies. Provide an overview of each of the four quadrants, review each quadrant in more detail and capture board comments.

- Identify roles and responsibilities for board members, including the board chair, board committees, and reporting authority.

- Review current job description of the GM/CEO and adjust as necessary for consistency with draft board governance policies. It is often helpful to prepare a draft revised GM/CEO job description in advance of the meeting—one that aligns more closely with the draft board governance policies.

- Identify draft Performance Metrics for use by the board in measuring performance of the GM/CEO, including topics to be reported on by the GM/CEO, items to monitor, and frequency of reporting. Providing the board with an example or two will go a long way in helping them understand how tracking metrics can help them monitor whether Strategic Direction is being achieved.

- Facilitate development of a board Stop-Doing List. This is a list of activities that the board may currently be doing that should be stopped altogether or delegated to the GM/CEO, thus allowing the board to focus on more productive activities. This exercise is often an eye-opener, especially for boards that are enmeshed in day-to-day operational issues of the organization.

- Identify areas where the board may wish to be continually educating itself in regards to macro trends or other areas that may strategically impact the organization. Examples might include commercial or residential growth, upcoming regulatory or legislative trends, recruiting and retention of staff, technology, benchmarking with peers, and so on.

Development of draft Performance Metrics for the GM/CEO can be an interesting exercise, especially if such metrics have not been previously developed or applied. It is often helpful to provide a sample reporting template to the board, perhaps filled in with items aligned with the SLP/TAP.

Prior to the third board work session, documentation should be provided to board members that includes information such as:

- Revised draft board governance policies
- Draft GM/CEO job description
- Draft board roles and responsibilities (This should align with the first quadrant of the model.)
- Draft GM/CEO performance monitoring plan

Board Governance Work Session No. 3
Objectives: Review, adjust, edit and finalize all previous deliverables.

Activities:
- Review and finalize draft board governance policies.
- Review and finalize the following draft documents:
  - GM/CEO job description
  - Roles and responsibilities of the board
  - GM/CEO Performance Metrics
  - Board continuing education objectives
  - Board Stop-Doing List
- Prepare an implementation schedule for board governance policies, including any necessary phase-in steps.

The implementation schedule may require some discussion. It is a natural tendency to want to go slow when implementing new policies. However, this can often be more disruptive to an organization than rapid implementation. Each board is different and each will have its own concerns about how fast to implement.

Final documents should be prepared for adoption by the board. These include:

- Board governance policies
- GM/CEO job description
- Roles and responsibilities of the board
- GM/CEO Performance Metrics
- Final board continuing education objectives
- Final board Stop-Doing List
- Implementation schedule

Implementing Board Governance Policies

If the board is like most we have worked with, it may experience difficulty implementing its new board governance policies. Typically this happens either because the board has not adequately identified "next steps" or because it lacks a mechanism to prevent it from slipping back into its former habits. Here are some ideas that other boards have found helpful when implementing their board governance policies.

Get Positioned for Success
- Establish a date for implementing the new set of policies. Putting it off or trying to implement in baby steps only results in lost momentum.
- Instruct legal counsel to review the final policies for compliance with local and state law. Make this a priority and be sure that it dovetails with the date established for implementation.
- Promote change within the boardroom. Consider implementing revisions to the standard board agenda. Suggestions include a regular report by the GM/CEO on status of implementation of the SLP, including a report on key Performance Metrics. If the board does not already do so, consider use of a consent agenda to efficiently cover routine items. Some boards have even changed the physical seating arrangement in the boardroom to emphasize that the GM/CEO is a direct report to the board.

Establish Processes for Maintaining Board Governance Policies
- Maintaining policy governance is the responsibility of the board, not staff. To this end, it is suggested that the board consider appointing one of its members to serve as a governance monitor

whose job is to help the board police itself on adherence to its board governance policies.

- The board must be the Change Agent of the organization. The board's job is to promote change and to drive it forward. Establishing, monitoring and, if necessary, changing Strategic Direction of the organization should be a primary work product of the board. To this end, the board should set processes in place so that it is constantly educating itself on a variety of issues that directly impact the Strategic Direction of the organization—things like changing growth patterns, upcoming regulations, or staff retention.

Constantly Monitor and Communicate Success
- In addition to setting Strategic Direction and educating itself, the board's third primary job should be to constantly monitor progress of the organization in achieving its objectives. As noted elsewhere, the GM/CEO has primary responsibility for implementing the directives of the board and should be tasked to report to the board on a regular basis.
- In addition to monitoring progress, the board should establish a process to regularly communicate success to customers, staff and outside stakeholders. Communication should include a statement of the Strategic Objective, what is being done to achieve it, and the value to the organization.

Index